Society Ending Events

The First 180 Days

By: Bob Gaskin

Dedication

This book is dedicated to the two most important people in my life. The first is my wife, Faith. Through good times and bad, through rich times and poor, through sickness and health, she has not left my side. She is my companion through life, and I am truly blessed to have her by my side.

The second is my daughter Carley. When the chips are down, I can always count on her to stand with me. In my opinion, she is my greatest accomplishment. I was blessed to have the opportunity to watch her grow through childhood and am proud of the woman she has become.

Special Thanks

There are so many people who were instrumental in bringing this book from a desired goal to a reality, far too many to list here. However, there were a few that I would be remise if I did not mention, a few who were very helpful in making the book a reality.

My Father, Bob Gaskin Sr., was the first to wake me up to the need to be prepared. He once told me that a prudent man is one that ensures his families survival and comfort through any eventuality. It is because of him that I began to prepare.

My best friend Keith Roberts. Keith has stood by my side since the fall of 1997. He has been there through highs and lows and has always stood beside me, even when I was wrong. In private, he would show me how I was wrong, but in public he was always by my side. I love him like a brother.

Scott Setter is my business associate in many ventures. While we have only known each other for roughly a year, he is someone I have come to trust and rely on.

Jerry Greer has recently come into my life. He started as a student in one of my seminars in 2012 and has quickly become a friend. He is someone I have come to respect. And in many ways has become the student that teaches the teacher. I look forward to learning more from this man I have come to respect.

Vincent Finelli is another person I have known for a short time but have come to respect. He has helped me to establish Black Dog Survival School in the Springfield market and further helped me to get my own radio show. He has been there whenever I have needed him and has come to be someone I respect.

Forward

It is my mission in life to spread the things that I know and learn to as many individuals as possible. It is my personal belief, that by the end of 2016, this planet will go through a series of events that will bring about a Society Ending Event here in the United States. It is also my belief that less than 6% of us will survive this Society Ending Event or the Great S.E.E. as I like to refer to it. As such, the more people I can convince to stop listening to the smoke screen rhetoric that is prominent in our media and propagated by fear mongering conspiracy theorists, and start researching for themselves to discover the truth of what lies ahead, the more people that will survive the Great SEE.

This book was written in a fashion as to be read as a conversation. My intention is not to lecture you or to tell you how to live your life or to make you believe as I do. As you read this book, my intent is that you feel as though we, you and I together, are having a conversation that will open your eyes to the truth and help you down the path of discovery.

I hope you enjoy the book.

Table of Contents

Chapter One

Chaos Theory

From Wikipedia, the free encyclopedia

Chaos theory is a field of study in mathematics, *with applications in several disciplines including* physics, engineering, economics, biology, *and* philosophy. *Chaos theory studies the behavior of* dynamical systems *that are highly sensitive to initial conditions, an effect which is popularly referred to as the* butterfly effect. *Small differences in initial conditions (such as those due to rounding errors in numerical computation) yield widely diverging outcomes for such dynamical systems, rendering long-term prediction impossible in general.[1] This happens even though these systems are* deterministic, *meaning that their future behavior is fully determined by their initial conditions, with no* random *elements involved.[2] In other words, the deterministic nature of these systems does not make them predictable.[3][4] This behavior is known as deterministic chaos, or simply chaos.*

Chaotic behavior can be observed in many natural systems, such as weather.[5][6] Explanation of such behavior may be sought through analysis of a chaotic mathematical model, *or through analytical techniques such as* recurrence plots **and** *Poincaré maps.*

Basically, Chaos Theory is the model in which we use to find the order, and even the beauty, in chaos. When we look closely enough, we will see patterns emerge. This is the greatest challenge facing Self Reliant Individuals today.

It is easy to get caught up in the conspiracy theories, news headlines, and political events. It is easy to get caught up in what is happening on our favorite sitcoms and reality shows. It is easy to get caught up in what our children are involved in and what health issues certain family members face. It is easy to get caught up in the latest neighborhood gossip of who is cheating on whom. It is easy to get caught up in the chaos that we allow to encompass our lives and command our thoughts. It is NOT so easy to stop, take a moment to catch our breath, and look closely into the chaos to find the patterns and watch them emerge. Sometimes, when we look closely, when we truly stare into the chaos, what we find is frightening to us. Other times, we see the beauty. Do not allow yourself to get trapped by your fear. Determine what it is that makes you afraid, educate yourself on that topic, and learn to understand it.

The internet is chaotic. It is filled with conspiracy theories propagated by Fear Mongers that profit from spreading that fear. If you wish to truly be informed, you need to look past the chaotic conspiracies and pear into the abyss that is the internet searching for the patterns. When you find the patterns, you will find the truth that lies within the beauty. This will be your "AH HA" moment. The moment when you stop listening to the chaotic conspiracies and discover the truth. The truth will horrify you. It will scare you more than any of the conspiracies ever had before. But it will also enlighten you to what lies ahead and allow you to better prepare. In this, you will find the means for which you will survive.

Think back to your childhood. As a child I played baseball. My memories of playing the game include my Mom in the stands cheering me on. My Dad was the head coach. For three years, from age 8 through 10, I played 2nd base for the Sugarland Bears. There was nothing like a warm spring day. Stepping toward the batter's box. A cool breeze blowing. The smells of spring baseball; of the freshly moved dirt, of the cut grass in the outfield, of the leather batting gloves I wore. Stepping up to the plate, digging my feet in for a solid stance, raising the bat over my right shoulder, staring down the pitcher over my left shoulder, willing him to throw that perfect pitch that would allow me to knock it out of the park. The pitcher would check first, then check third. Once satisfied, he would look at me, confirm the signal from the catcher, and then stare me right in the eyes. He would begin his wind up, lean forward, around came his arm, he releases the ball, my eyes follow the ball, and at just the right moment I swing. Crack!

Great pitch, not a bad swing, and the ball is gone. Those are my memories of youth baseball.

Now let's look at that memory in a different light. When the pitcher checked 1st and 3rd, I knew the wind up was about to begin. I knew to focus on the pitchers arm. Once the windup was complete, I knew the pitch was soon to follow. Focusing on the pitch I was able to watch the ball as it left the pitchers hand until it crossed just the right spot for me to begin my swing. But what if, just before the pitcher checked 1st, the Umpire yelled my name and startled me to the point where I focused on him instead of the pitcher? I would have missed the wind up. I would not have been paying attention to the ball and would not have been able to begin my swing at just the right time. I would have missed the ball if I turned away from the Umpire in time to realize the pitch had left the mound, or I would have been hit in the back of the head if I were still focusing on the Umpire. In baseball, the only way to score is to make it to base. The only way to make it to base is to hit the ball. And the only way to hit the ball is to keep your focus on the pitcher as he goes through the motions.

I liken the Umpire in this story to the conspiracy theory fear mongers. I liken the pitcher to the disasters we are facing, and the ball as the catalyst that brings about the Society Ending Event that we all fear and are preparing for. And I liken missing the ball to death. Those of us that choose to pay attention to the Umpire screaming about things such as FEMA Camps, FEMA Coffins, the Economical Collapse, a Nationwide Pandemic, Mega Earthquakes, Rising Oceans, and the threat of Nuclear Armageddon will miss the ball. We will strike out. We will not survive the Society Ending Event because we will miss the telltale signs that it is upon us. We will die. Or worse, we will survive long enough to see those loved ones that depended on us die due to our lack of understanding, education, and preparedness. Those of us that tune out the screaming Umpire and focus on what is coming, who know what events follow other specific events, will survive and see our loved ones survive because we are prepared.

FEMA Camps. We really love to go on and on about how evil FEMA Camps are. Many of us even call them Americas Concentration Camps. Ironically enough, those of us that continue to harp about the FEMA Camps are the same ones that continue to criticize FEMA for its lack of preparedness in the wake of such storms as Hurricanes Andrew, Katrina, and Sandy. We don't take the time to research the FEMA Camps enough to get past the conspiracies to realize that the sole mission of these camps is to provide a secure, climate controlled environment for those that become refugees in the aftermath of a catastrophic disaster. It is true that "Absolute Power Corrupts Absolutely". In the aftermath of a Society Ending Event, the commandants of a FEMA Family

Relocation Facility will have a well trained security force, plenty of food, and absolute power. But short of a Society Ending Event, the FEMA Family Relocation Centers will continue to perform their primary mission: To securely house and provide for refugees from a catastrophic disaster. FEMA Camps were not created to control the masses once a police state occurs. They were created to take care of the masses following a disaster.

FEMA Coffins. This is my favorite conspiracy. It is also the conspiracy that is easily overcome with simple logic. Why do we fear the FEMA Coffins? Because we fear death. Many of us are convinced that at some time in the near future the United States of America will once again face a massive pandemic that will reach at least 35% of the population. Many of us prepare for the day when we will not be able to leave our homes without the use of gas masks and chemical suits. In fact, the latest polls show that roughly 1 in every 9 Americans believes we will face a pandemic and are preparing for it by stockpiling protective masks, clothing, and gloves as well as various antibiotics and other medications. If we are so convinced that we are facing a pandemic in the near future, and we are convinced that there will be mass deaths as a result, then why do we find fault with FEMA for having the same beliefs and criticize them for preparing for it? If 1 out of 3 Americans dies as a result of a pandemic or other disaster, what is the government supposed to do with all the bodies? It makes sense to me to have tens of thousands of coffins that will hold four to six adult bodies just for this issue! Personally, I am thankful that the government has made preparations for the aftermath of what so many of us are convinced is imminent. Wherein can we find fault with this?

Intentional Economic Collapse. I travel all over the country teaching Preparedness Seminars and being a vendor at gun shows and preparedness expos. I spend several hours every weekend talking to people from all walks of life, from school teachers to doctors to farmers, to law enforcement professionals. One of the most fascinating things I hear from them is that they believe that the "Financial Elite" are planning on crashing the world's currencies, specifically the US Dollar, to bring about a global economic collapse so they can bring about a One World Currency. Let's look at this logically for a moment. The financial elite are the financial elite because they have the majority of the money. If they bring about the devaluing of that money, they will be just as broke as the rest of us. This would cause them to lose the status of being "Financially Elite". Therefore, they would be the catalyst for their own demise and would no longer be elite enough to bring about the One World Currency.

Planet X. Wormwood. Nibiru. The Great Destroyer. The beauty of the Bible is that it is based on Faith. In order to believe the Bible, you have to have Faith that it is the sole word of God. Ironically enough, we the advance of modern technology, the Science and Archeological Communities have proven the majority of the Old Testament. We have found Noah's Ark, the Ark of the Covenant, Solomon's Temple; the list goes on and on. Ironically enough, the same scientific, archeological, and historical data that proves the Old Testament is the exact same data that proves the existence of Planet X and the Annanuchi. So when I am confronted by Christians who are concerned with the theory of Planet X, I like to ask them which they believe in the most; the Bible or Planet X.

Every culture, society, or religion that existed 3500 years ago all have the same three things in common; the creation of the first Homo Sapiens Adam and Eve, Noah's Flood, and the End of the World. If you take a few days and study the scientific, historic, and archeological data, then add in the Biblical timeline, you find that roughly every 3647 years all 88 cycles the earth goes through happen within the same nine months. It is all cyclic and obviously survivable. If this great natural disaster was not survivable, humans would not be here today and you would not be reading this book. The question is, have you built your ark? I ask this because it is my belief that we are in the 3646th year of the cycle. You see, the Mayans never predicted the "End of the World". They forecasted that at the end of their calendar the world would face the end of an age. On December

23rd, 2012 at roughly 1100 UTC, our solar system along with several others completed a 255 million year cycle around the center of the Milky Way. This was a major event that the majority of us missed because we were so focused on the media hype about the End of the World. What we should have been focusing on was the location of the planet in the universe. Of the great universal plasma belt we were entering. But more importantly of the Natural Events that are have already become extremely problematic in the world and are going to continue to do so over the next few years. Planet X or the Bible? I choose to believe in the Bible.

Are you beginning to see a pattern here?

The internet is a wonderful creation. Never before in history have we, as a generation, literally had all the information in the world just a click away. Unfortunately, it is also the ultimate Chaos! Every one of us now has the ability to have an International Voice. A platform for which we can rant on and on about what we believe. Remember the definition of the Chaos Theory? You have to stare into the chaos and search for the patterns to see the beauty of the entire picture. Stop searching the internet for the latest conspiracy theories. Stop focusing on those things that cannot be proven, and even if they could, you can do nothing about. Look past the conspiracies and search for the patterns that will help you to discover the truth. When you find them, you will know what to prepare for and how to survive what is coming. If you truly want to survive the upcoming Society Ending Events, you must be educated on what they are, watchful of their foretelling events, and prepared to weather the storm.

Chapter Two

Destructive Scenarios

There are many Destructive Scenarios that we should be concerned with here in the United States. Some are man-made, and some are natural disasters. The ones we are going to look at in this chapter are the ones that are the most prevalent at this time. Ironically enough, as we go through this chapter it will become clear that many of the scenarios that are at the root of conspiracies are actually the byproduct, or subsequent event, to the Society Ending Event. At the same time, the majority of the Society Ending Events are subsequent events to other events. By knowing which events lead to other events, you will become aware as to what signs to watch for and what events to prepare for.

Picture yourself sitting in a professional basketball arena. You are up in the nose bleed section. On the basketball court floor, someone has taken months to lay out hundreds of thousands of multi colored dominoes. The dominoes are strategically placed so that when the first one is toppled it will start a chain of events whereby the other dominoes will continue to fall to reveal a grand picture.

Being in the nose bleed section, you are not able to see, nor hear, the first domino fall. But as more and more chains of dominoes fall and the noise of them hitting the hardwood floor reaches a maximum, you are able to see and hear them. Eventually, you will see the picture start to form. And as you sit there in awe of what is happening on the basketball court floor, your mind focused on the overall picture, it will not occur to you to consider the hundreds upon hundreds of hours it took someone to carefully place each domino. Nor, no matter how hard you try or how much you focus, will you be able to watch one particular domino fall. Some of the dominoes falling cause another to fall. Some cause up to three to fall starting three chains from the previous one. Some are the final domino in the chain and have no subsequent dominoes falling. If we try to focus on one specific domino, we will miss the entire picture unfolding before our eyes. More to the point, if we are not watching the entire picture unfold, we will not know when a specific domino is to fall.

This is what we are currently facing. We do not realize that the Society Ending Event is not the first domino to fall, but is actually a single domino somewhere in the middle of the field that follows another domino falling and also has the potential to cause another domino to fall. Meaning, that when we face a Society Ending Event, it will be the result of a previous event or events. The things we fear the most, things like economic collapse and pandemics, will be subsequent events to a Society Ending

Event. This means that if you are only watching for the end results, you will miss the event itself and therefore will not survive the event.

The focus of this chapter is to get you, the reader, to understand what we are really facing and to start watching for it. This will allow you to understand the event, prepare for the event, prepare your family for the event, have a plan for responding to the event, and survive the event.

Coronal Mass Ejection (CME). Many people have a misunderstanding in the difference between CMEs, Solar Flares, and Coronal Solar Radiation. Solar Flares are actually good for our planet and are needed to strengthen our Magnetosphere. CMEs are bad for our planet because they cause the sun facing side of the magnetosphere to flatten and cause the opposite side to elongate. And coronal radiation is never good for our planet.

Yes, there exists the possibility that with the way our society has grown so dependent on technology, a powerful CME could take out our satellites and even our power grid. Yes, a powerful CME could be the event that causes a Society Ending Event.

Coronal mass ejection

From Wikipedia, the free encyclopedia

A <u>coronal mass ejection (CME)</u> is a massive burst of solar wind and magnetic fields rising above the solar corona or being released into space.[1] Coronal mass ejections are often associated with other forms of solar activity, most notably solar flares, but a causal relationship has not been established. Most ejections originate from active regions on the Sun's surface, such as groupings of sunspots associated with frequent flares. Near solar maxima the Sun produces about three CMEs every day, whereas near solar minima there is about one CME every five days.[2]

Solar Flares. Solar flares help to strengthen our magnetosphere. This is why they are good. While most people fear solar flares due to mistaking their effect to be the same as that of a CME, solar flares are something that our planet needs to survive and maintain our magnetosphere, and atmosphere. While the majority of solar flares are of the "good" variety, there is the potential of a massive solar flare that could cripple our technology and power grid.

Solar flare

From Wikipedia, the free encyclopedia

A <u>solar flare</u> is a sudden brightening observed over the Sun's surface or the solar limb, which is interpreted as a large energy release of up to 6 × 10^{25} joules of energy (about a sixth of the total energy output of the Sun each second or 160,000,000,000 megatons of TNT equivalent, over

25,000 times more energy than released from the impact of Comet Shoemaker–Levy 9 with Jupiter). They are mainly followed by a colossal coronal mass ejection also known as a CME.[1] The flare ejects clouds of electrons, ions, and atoms through the corona of the sun into space. These clouds typically reach Earth a day or two after the event.[2] The term is also used to refer to similar phenomena in other stars, where the term stellar flare applies.

Solar flares affect all layers of the solar atmosphere (photosphere, chromosphere, and corona), when the plasma medium is heated to tens of millions of kelvins the electrons, protons, and heavier ions are accelerated to near the speed of light. They produce radiation across the electromagnetic spectrum at all wavelengths, from radio waves to gamma rays, although most of the energy is spread over frequencies outside the visual range and for this reason the majority of the flares are not visible to the naked eye and must be observed with special instruments. Flares occur in active regions around sunspots, where intense magnetic fields penetrate the photosphere to link the corona to the solar interior. Flares are powered by the sudden (timescales of minutes to tens of minutes) release of magnetic energy stored in the corona. The same energy releases may produce coronal mass ejections (CME), although the relation between CMEs and flares is still not well established.

X-rays and UV radiation emitted by solar flares can affect Earth's ionosphere and disrupt long-range radio communications. Direct radio emission at decimetric wavelengths may disturb operation of radars and other devices operating at these frequencies.

Solar flares were first observed on the Sun by Richard Christopher Carrington and independently by Richard Hodgson in 1859[3] as localized visible brightenings of small areas within a sunspot group. Stellar flares have also been observed on a variety of other stars.

The frequency of occurrence of solar flares varies, from several per day when the Sun is particularly "active" to less than one every week when the Sun is "quiet", following the 11-year cycle (the solar cycle). Large flares are less frequent than smaller ones.

The Importance. So, why are we so concerned with CMEs and solar flares. The answer is simple. Not only do these events have the ability to bring about a Society Ending Event, they are also the catalyst for other natural disaster; specifically volcanoes and earthquakes.

Science has recently proven that seismic and volcanic activity is directly related to extreme solar activity such as solar flares and CMEs. Meaning, that directly following CMEs or extreme solar flare activity, we see an uptick in seismic and volcanic activity. Since the two are directly related to increased solar activity, we recognize that the more realistic threat to our infrastructure from CMEs or Solar Flares comes in the form of volcanoes and earth quakes.

Volcanoes in the United States. While a volcanic eruption is not something that occurs every day, it is a threat that has been recently growing in probability. There are many people in the United States that believe that we will see an eruption of the Mega Volcano at Yellowstone sometime in their lifetime. While this is a credible threat, it is unlikely that we will see it in our lifetime as a standalone event. I say stand alone, because the threat is increased when you work into the probability calculator the additional threat of seismic activity in the region coupled with a massive solar flare storm or CME.

Earthquakes. Here lies our greatest natural threat disaster. Due to our position in the universe, coupled with the decrease in solar maximum and the slowing down of the sun, the threat level of earthquakes is gaining. At the time this book was written, February and March 2013, we have seen a major uptick in seismic activity. All of the nature precursors and indicators exist to point toward a mega quake (7.0 or higher) here in the United States. When this happens, the resulting affects of the quake would destroy our economy, cause wide spread panic, and would bring about such devastation that we would not survive as a society. Meaning, that a mega quake in the United States would be the catalyst that would quickly bring about a Society Ending Event. It would destroy our infrastructure, destroy our economy, create massive civil unrest and chaos, cause a pandemic, and basically destroy life as we know it.

Rising Oceans. This is a topic that I thoroughly enjoy. Yes, our northern polar ice is melting. Yes, the Northern Hemisphere is experiencing Global Warming. However, the Southern Hemisphere is experiencing Global Cooling. This is the result of Global Dimming, which is the result of the Sun slowing down its spin, which is a precursor to the Earth experiencing a wobble shift. I have said all that to say that while we are experiencing massive ice melting in the northern pole, we are also watching large amounts of ice forming in the southern pole. In fact, in 2012, we say an increase in southern polar ice at a ratio of 1.6 to that of the decrease in the northern polar ice.

Yes, our shore lines are decreasing. They are doing so as a result of rising oceans. However, without the impact into the formula of an external force such as a meteor or asteroid, the oceans cannot rise to the point of quick increase to create a devastating event. The threat to our coastlines comes in the form of tsunami and external threats.

Global dimming

From Wikipedia, the free encyclopedia

Global dimming is the gradual reduction in the amount of global direct irradiance **at the** Earth's **surface that was observed for several decades after the start of systematic measurements in the 1950s. The effect varies by location, but worldwide it has been estimated to be of the order of a 4% reduction over the three decades from 1960–1990. However, after discounting an anomaly caused by the eruption of** Mount Pinatubo **in 1991, a very slight reversal in the overall trend has been observed.**[1]

Global dimming is thought to have been caused by an increase in particulates **such as** sulfate aerosols **in the atmosphere due to human action.**

It has interfered with the hydrological cycle **by reducing evaporation and may have reduced rainfall in some areas. Global dimming also creates a** cooling **effect that may have partially masked the effect of** greenhouse gases **on** global warming.

Solar maximum

From Wikipedia, the free encyclopedia

Solar maximum or solar max is a normal period of greatest solar activity in the 11 year solar cycle **of the** Sun. **During solar maximum, large numbers of** sunspots **appear and the sun's irradiance output**

grows by about 0.1%.[1] *The increased energy output of solar maxima can impact global climate and recent studies have shown some correlation with regional weather patterns.*

At solar maximum, the Sun's magnetic field lines are the most distorted due to the magnetic field on the solar equator rotating at a slightly faster pace than at the solar poles.[citation needed] *The solar cycle takes an average of about 11 years to go from one solar maximum to the next, with an observed variation in duration of 9 to 14 years for any given solar cycle.*

Large solar flares often occur during a maximum. For example, the Solar storm of 1859 struck the Earth with such intensity that the northern lights could be seen as far south as Rome, approximately 42° north of the equator

Solar minimum

From Wikipedia, the free encyclopedia

Solar minimum is the period of least solar activity in the 11 year solar cycle of the sun. During this time, sunspot and solar flare activity diminishes, and often does not occur for days at a time. The date of the minimum is described by a smoothed average over 12 months of sunspot activity, so identifying the date of the solar minimum usually can only happen 6 months after the minimum takes place. Solar minima are not generally correlated with changes in climate but recent studies have shown a correlation with regional weather patterns.

Solar minimum is contrasted with the solar maximum, where there may be hundreds of sunspots.

Geothermal Nuclear War. This is the second most credible manmade threat the United States is currently facing. While the threat of nuclear Armageddon has existed since the 1950's, there was always a sense of normalcy in the idea of MAD, Mutually Assured Destruction. However, since nations in the Middle East started to acquire the technology to create nuclear warheads, the threat level has changed. We are no longer dealing with a nuclear arms race that consists of two nations who realized that by destroying the other they were destroying themselves. We now face a very real and very credible threat of nations entering the nuclear arms race that do not care about their own destruction, as long as they destroy their enemy. We are facing the threat from three fronts.

Front One is North Korea. At this time of this writing, the threat of violent aggression from North Korea is the highest it has been since the 1950's. In the midst of this heightened threat, we realize that North Korea is extremely close to developing a nuclear warhead.

Front Two is Iran. The belief of the Iranian Leaders is that they are embarking on a Holy War that will end with the emergence of a new Ottoman Empire wherein Sharia Law will become Global Law. They are convinced that the only roadblock to their achievement of this goal is the destruction of the United States. This is the nation to watch for as the next credible threat of nuclear war.

Front Three comes in a more passive aggressive form. Russia and China. While neither of the two countries is threatening a global conflict, both have firmly stated their intent to stand by Iran. Meaning that a conflict with Iran will not be a localized conflict. Russia and China both will stand by Iran which means this conflict will become a global conflict. It is my belief that should this happen, we will firmly face a nuclear conflict.

EMP. And here lies the single most credible and probable man made Society Ending Event facing the United States. Both Korea and Iran have practiced launching missiles from platform on container ships. Both nations have stated their desire to bring violent conflict to the United States. Both nations are aware of the fact that an EMP, detonated at roughly 8000 feet over the central United States would bring our country to a halt. And let's face reality. Without our electrical infrastructure, we are done.

Chapter Three

The First 180 Days

The first 180 days following a Society Ending Event are the most critical. Studies have been done by Military and Governmental Agencies all over the world and the conclusions are all the same. When the United States of America faces a Society Ending Event, 86-94% of the population will not survive the first 180 days. Let's look at this a different way. Nineteen out of twenty people you know will not be alive six months after the Society Ending Event. Nineteen out of twenty!

Are you sure you want to survive?

I ask that question because the answer to that question is the single most critical determination you can have as to how to prepare and for what you are preparing. For many, when they read this section, they will immediately answer that question with a yes. They will do so without really thinking about the question or the consequences of what will follow. Many of us have already progressed through the five stages of preparing and find ourselves at the final stage. This makes it near impossible to consider the ramifications of the answer to that question.

Five Stages of Preparation

Stage One: This is our moment of awareness. At some point in our lives, someone, something, or some event made us open our eyes to the reality of how fragile our society is. This moment of awareness is considered to be stage one. This is the shortest of all stages because once you hit stage one, you immediately move to stage two. For some, it could last weeks. For me, it was about 3 hours.

Stage Two: Fearful Purchasing. We have all been there. Those days just after our moment of awareness wherein we started buying anything and everything that we thought we would need to survive the "End of the World". Food that we would normally not eat was purchased simply because it had a long shelf life. We bought firearms we had zero knowledge of and made sure we had all the accessories and plenty of ammo. We bought tents and put together Bug Out Bags (BOB) without really knowing what we needed to put into them. This is the stage where we are most susceptible to those that profit from generating and spreading fear. A side note for those that are just now entering Stage Two. Before you spend a gross amount of money on items you do not need, please do two things. One, use the list in the back of this book as a guide, not a manual. While I believe it is the most comprehensive list available today, it is only a guide and is generalized for the entire nation. You will need to customize it to fit your particular geographical location. Two, find a level headed, trustworthy person who is also into preparedness and ask them for their guidance.

Stage Three: Structured Preparation. This is the stage where you become obsessed with research. You are no longer overwhelmed by the sheer magnitude of fear that prompted you to start prepping. You research everything you can until you think you have researched it all only to find out that there is more to research. While the downside is that your obsession grows, the upside is that you are more structured and organized in your preps. You become increasingly aware of what your family will truly need to make it through several years and studiously plan and purchase to get to a comfort level that you think is sufficient. You no longer purchase an item because of its expiration date, but instead because of its value to you or your family following a Society Ending Event.

Stage Four: Expert Level. With most of us, about the time we think we have researched all we need to know, we also develop a sense of superiority. Due to the level of preparations we have made, when we encounter people who are just getting started and are in stage one or two, we feel a sense of superiority toward them. We feel we have become experts. This is mainly because so many of them are asking for our help and advice. These could be family members or just close friends. It is typically in stage four that we realize we no longer need to be a part of someone else's group and under their authority so we set out to start our own group. This way of thinking can be very bad for us. We sometimes alienate those people that have helped us get to the level we are at. My advice to you, tread carefully. Remember, even if you have your own retreat and have founded your own group, once the SHTF, you do not want to be alone. There is power and strength in numbers. Do not alienate your friends or group that you were formally a member of. Keep in close contact with them and if you have formed your own group at your own retreat, it is wise to realize that you may someday need them. Work out future trade negotiations now, before the SHTF.

Stage Five: The Danger Zone. Do not fall into the trap. Self Reliant Individuals that have succumbed to stage five can be very dangerous. These are the people who are actually looking forward to the SHTF. When you encounter these people, do not share too much with them and be very careful about letting them into your group. As we will discuss in the following pages, a lot of people are going to die when we face a Society Ending Event. Any person that claims they want it to happen is someone who cares only for themselves and not for their fellow man. This is a person that you do not want knowing where your supplies are stored or what you security situation is. If you find yourself getting to the point where you are constantly thinking about, dreaming about, or looking forward to the SHTF, then you have reached stage five. My suggestion to you is to take a serious break from your research and preparations. Do not fall into this trap.

Reality

There are many myths and misconceptions in the Self Reliant World. We have watched every movie and read every book we could concerning the End of the World as We Know It (TEOTWAWKI). Do not get me wrong. I have watched them or read them as well. I have acquired many great ideas from them and gained much knowledge. The downside to these books and movies is that, in most cases, the main character survives. A great book or movie is one in which the reader/viewer becomes so submersed in the story that they can visualize themselves as the main character. This is what I call the "Rambo" affect. We become so immersed in the story and the main character that we develop a sense of superiority toward others. We begin to think that since we have prepared for this, we will survive. Unfortunately, we will not all survive. Some of us will simply be in the wrong place at the wrong time and will not survive. Just because you own an AR15 does not mean that you have the intestinal fortitude to use it. Having all the latest and greatest survival products will not insure your survival. You have to know what to expect and mentally and physically prepare for it.

What to expect.

It seems that among the Prepper Community, the most prominent threat is believed to be an EMP. We all know the scenario as it is portrayed in the books and in the movies. Unfortunately, the reality of what would follow is much worse. History has showed us that the optimal time for a terror attack is 9:22 AM local time. The reason for this is that from 9 AM to 5 PM, the bulk of us are at work. If we are attacked during this time when adults are at work and children are in school, the average person's primary concern will not be in repelling the attack, but in the safety of our family.

Day One

Time and again we have seen how quickly society can crumble. Katrina and Sandy both showed us how unprepared our society is for a catastrophic disaster. They have both also showed us how quickly we lose our civility when our way of life temporarily ends.

The first day following an EMP will be more devastating than you can imagine. Sure, the lights will be out. What else?

Every day, there are over 28,000 commercial flights in the United States, the majority of which are in the air between 6 AM and Midnight. During an 18 hour day, this is an average of over 1500 flights per hour.

The average number of seats on a plane is 106. This means that at any point during the day, there are over 150,000 people in the air. When an EMP hits, these people will not survive. Additionally, the latest studies show that an estimated 125,000 people will die from planes falling from the skies. Totaling over 275,000 people dying as a result of the planes falling out of the sky.

Every day, there is an average of 630,000 people on life support in hospitals in the United States. An EMP would not only destroy the power grid, but back-up generators as well. It is believed that the majority of these 630,000 people would not survive the first 24 hours.

Over the last decade, we have seen the effects on our natural gas lines from power surges that occur just prior to an overload. Experts now agree that should the United States get hit with an EMP, the majority of our gas relay switches and pumps would explode. This would cause major destruction to our natural gas infrastructure. Every city in the United States would experience thousands of natural gas explosions. Latest statistics show that 1 in 7 houses would be in the impact zone of these explosions and would catch fire. Additionally, it is believed that the power surge caused by the EMP that would bring down the electrical grid would cause 1 in 6 houses to catch fire. Without critical services like Fire Departments, Police, and EMTs, the expected casualties from fires and explosions on day one are over 1.3 million people.

On an average day in the United States there are over 32 million vehicles on the interstate. It is estimated that at any point in time during the day, there is an average of 9.6 million people in motor vehicles. Unfortunately, when the electrical system goes out on a car or truck, the vehicle does not simply roll to a stop. The driver will lose control of the steering, the brakes, and the gas. Vehicles will crash into each other. People will run into each other or other objects. The general belief among experts is that if the United States were to get hit with an EMP, 4.3 million people would either die immediately, or within the next 48 hours as a result of traffic accidents.

There are roughly 1.7 million beds in nursing homes in the United States, with an average occupancy rate of 86%. This means that there is an average of 1,462,000 people in nursing homes. An average of 81% of them are on some type of medically assisted living such as life support, intravenous feeding, etc., and they are less than 12 hours from death. This means that within the first 24 hours following an EMP, an additional 1,184,220 people will die due to lack of medical care.

That is a total of 7.7 million people dying the first 24 hours following an EMP. This does not even take into account the human response to the EMP.

Latest studies show that the general belief among experts is that during the first 24 hours following an EMP, over 300,000 people will die from self inflicted wounds. An additional 2.1 million will die from violence. Last, an additional 700,000 will die from injuries sustained during panic caused riots.

The expected number of deaths in the United States in the first 24 hours following an EMP is 10.8 million people. To bring it closer to home, that is 3% of the population of the United States, or one in 35 people.

Day Two through Day Twenty-One

The following is a list of what the experts believe we should expect from day 2 through day 21 following an EMP.

- 1.6 million people will die from exposure
- 6.3 million people will die from thirst
- 9.8 million people will die from starvation
- 4.7 million people will die from lack of critical services
- 3.2 million people will die from suicide
- 22 million people will die from violence

The total number of deaths expected during days two through twenty-one is 47.6 million people. Combined with the expected deaths from the first 24 hours and we are looking at a loss of life in the United States of 58.4 million Americans during the first three weeks. To bring this closer to home, that is less than one in every six Americans.

These are not the statistics of some kid blogging away on his computer at night on some conspiracy website. These statistics come from government websites. If you will take the time to stare into the chaotic internet long enough to look past the conspiracies and search for the truth, you will find it. It is there waiting for you.

The safest place for you and your family is in your home or retreat. If you cannot get to your safe place within the first 7 days, the safest thing for you to do is to get your family, get home, and bug in.

Day Twenty-Two through day Forty

By day twenty-two, we have already seen a loss of life in the United States of 58.4 million people. This will leave the population of the United States roughly 270 million people. Keep in mind that in 2007, for the first time in history, greater than fifty percent of the world population lived in major cities. By day twenty-two, the vast majority of the people living in urban areas will have already fled to the country. There is a belief that exists among the experts that by day twenty-two, an estimated 140 million people will be displaced from their homes having fled to the countryside mistakenly believing that they will find food in the country.

A friend of mine lives in a suburb of North Atlanta. We were talking one day and he explained where he lived and asked if I thought he was in a good area to wait out the first 180 days. He is roughly 20 miles or so north of Atlanta and within a few miles of the interstate. As we were talking, I pointed out two things to him.

First, all the experts agree that following a catastrophic event, the more normal a lifestyle you can maintain for your family, the better off they will be. For example, if you have school age children who are unable to attend school due to the disaster, make sure that you spend a few hours a day with them doing school work. This is part of their routine and it is important to keep things as routine as possible around you. This is another reason for bugging in as opposed to bugging out. To a child, their home is their safe place. Being at home equates to them as being safe. Being safe limits fear which in turn limits anxiety.

The second thing I pointed out to him showed the reason why he should not stay in that area and to have a location he could go to. I told him that 5.2 million people live in Atlanta and surrounding communities. As food supplies start to diminish and the exodus begins from Atlanta, if only ten percent of the population headed north, that would equate to 520,000 people. If only ten percent of them left the interstate near his exit that would equate to 52,000 people. If only ten percent of those people headed in the direction of his home that would equate to 5,200 people. If only ten percent of those people made it to his neighborhood that would mean that he would have to defend his home from 520 hungry and desperate people. Then I asked him what he thought the odds were that at each of those junctions, only as few as ten percent would head his way. You could see the light bulb pop above his head. That afternoon, my friend realized that even though he had plenty of stockpiles of supplies for himself and his family, the reality of the situation was that he stood a very real possibility of having to defend his family against thousands of hungry and desperate people.

When you work up a mathematical equation taking into account historical data from previous societal collapses, and add to the equation our nation's dependency on technology and the ability to survive in normal times with only a couple days worth of food in your house, you find a very disturbing reality. What you find is that by day twenty-two, the average person has lost all sense of civility. You realize that the average person will now do things they never thought they were capable of doing under "normal" circumstances. This means that violence will greatly escalate during the second dying time.

Today, our nation has grown increasingly dependent on medication. So much so that one in five Americans are on some type of mind altering medication. That equates to roughly twenty percent of the remaining 270 million Americans being on some type of mind altering medication with, on average, a thirty day supply. With 52 million of the remaining 270 million Americans running out of their medication that treats them for anxiety, depression, ADHD, ADD, and a plethora of other ailments, when these medications start to run out we will see an increase in violence and suicide.

Additionally, other medications will begin to run out as well. It is generally known that the majority of insulin dependent diabetics will not last the first 40 days following a Society Ending Event. What most people do not take into account is the additional eight percent of the population that is on a regimented life sustaining medical treatment. For example, people with Crones disease that have to have monthly treatments will not survive long once they have restricted access to medicine, their diet drastically changes, and their stress levels are greatly increased.

The following statistics show what the projects are for the second dying time.

- 13.1 million people will die from exposure
- 4.9 million people will die from thirst
- 23.7 million people will die from starvation

- 17.2 million people will die from lack of critical services
- 37.4 million will die from lack of necessary medication
- 9.6 million people will die from suicide
- 57 million people will die from violence

If these statistics are accurate, from day twenty-two through day forty, 162.9 million people will die. That is roughly half the current population of the United States. To bring it closer to home, that is roughly one out of every two people.

By day forty following an EMP, the expectations are that 221.3 million Americans will have died. Two out of every three Americans will have perished. Can you imagine what this will look like? By day forty, critical services will be a thing from the past. When we think about a post society collapse world, we all readily recognize that the Law Enforcement and Fire Departments will no longer exist. What many of us seem to miss is that other critical services will no longer exist as well. For example, there will not be EMTs, Paramedics, or Coroners. Which brings about the question, "Who will dispose of the bodies?" Two out of every three Americans, lying dead in their cars, homes, offices, front yards, back yards. Who will dispose of the bodies? The answer is simple. There will be no one to dispose of the majority of the bodies. This is the major cause of the next dying time.

Day Forty through Day One Hundred Eighty

By day forty following a Society Ending Event, the population of the United States has been reduced by 221.3 million people. This will leave a population of roughly 113 million people. Depending on what season the Society Ending Event occurs, will depend on when the third dying time starts. This is where the mathematical equation takes a serious turn.

If the Society Ending Event takes place during late fall or early winter, then the weather will play into the equation as concerns a longer time before the disease begins to spread. Unfortunately, when people are hungry, tired, and cold, they tend to become desperate quicker. Meaning that with the Society Ending Event taking place in the late fall or early winter, more people will die from exposure and violence than will if the Society Ending Event occurred during the summer.

If the Society Ending Event occurs during the spring or summer, fewer people will die from exposure after the forty day mark, but the disease caused from all of the dead bodies will spread quicker.

Either way, it is believed that during this final dying time that will take place sometime between day forty and day one hundred and eighty, it is believed that between 76 million and 92 million people will die from violence, exposure, and disease.

By day one hundred and eighty, eighty-six to ninety-four percent of the population of the United States will have died. Being someone who always plans for the worst and hopes for the best, I have to look at the worst case scenario in all things. With these numbers, the worst case scenario is that ninety-four percent of the population will not survive the first six months. That is nineteen out of every twenty people. This means that if I, my wife, my daughter, and my parents survive, ninety-five other people will die. It also means that statistically, nineteen out of every twenty people will die.

On the next page, I have a little exercise for you to do. Nobody will see the results other than you. Do the exercise or don't do the exercise, the choice is yours. If you do it, please make the most of it. Be honest with yourself and try not to curtail the results.

In the space below, fill in the blanks with the twenty people you are closest to. These names can be your spouse, children, aunts, uncles, grandparents, friends, neighbors. You can even put the name of your high school sweet heart if you want. But please complete the list.

_____   _____

_____   _____

_____   _____

_____   _____

_____   _____

_____   _____

_____   _____

_____   _____

_____   _____

_____   _____

Now, in the space below, please randomly choose a number between one and twenty.

_____

To complete the exercise, tear a piece of paper into twenty pieces and number each piece of paper one through twenty. Put the pieces into a bowl and randomly select one piece. Then circle the name on the list that equates to the number on the piece of paper. Statistically, that is the only person on the list that will survive the first one hundred and eighty days.

Put the piece of paper back into the bowl and draw another piece. If the number on the new piece is the same number that you wrote down for the second exercise, then congratulations. That is the statistical chance that you would be one of the six percent that is still alive at day one hundred and eighty-one.

As you read the next chapter, the importance of this exercise will sink in.

Chapter Four

Developing the Survivor Mindset

Do you want to survive?

Are you still answering yes? Do you really want to survive? Let's face it; a Society Ending Event is the extreme end of worst case scenarios. When people say, "What is the worst that could happen?" The answer is always a Society Ending Event. If the worst case for a Society Ending Event is that ninety-four percent of the population is dead, do you really want to be one of the six percent that survives? You should be thinking about this long and hard. Imagine a world wherein there is no electricity, critical services have stopped, the grocery store shelves are empty, you are living day to day off of your skills, and nineteen out of every twenty people have died. Every time you enter a building or home you find dead people. There exists no government, no order, and no rule of law. Every person you come into contact with could possibly try to kill you for what meager belongings you have. In the back of your head you have to ask yourself if that person wants to hurt you, kill you, or even eat you. Forming new relationships will be tricky at best because you will have learned to not trust anyone. If you are an average person, by this time you will have run out of supplies and will have had to make choices you did not think you would ever have to make and do things you would never have thought you would have to do.

There is a greater than eighty percent chance that if you have survived the first one hundred and eighty days following a Society Ending Event you will have had to take another human life at least once.

Imagine the worst nightmare you have ever had, add to it the most gruesome movie you have ever watched and then multiply by one thousand. This is the world you will find yourself living in if you survive the first one hundred and eighty days. By day one hundred and eighty-two, statically, you would have watched your spouse, your children, and your entire family die.

Do you want to survive?

If, after doing the previous exercises, reading the previous page, and truly thinking long and hard about the question, you still want to be one of the six percent, then keep reading this book.

If the answer to the question is now no, do not be dismayed. It's okay. There does not exist in every person the ability to cope with that kind of stress and loss. If your decision is to not survive, then enjoy the time you have left. Take a vacation. Spend time with your family. Enjoy life. And please give this book to someone you know that practices the Self Reliant Lifestyle.

If you are still reading, then I congratulate you. So far you have had to face who you truly are and decide that your life is worth living no matter what the circumstances are in which you have to live it. You have already climbed the first stair toward developing the survivor mindset. So now you are ready to climb the remaining stairs.

Hard Choices. Here the difficulty begins. The average person has led a life of comfort where the lines between right and wrong are always clearly divided. When faced with a decision to make, you simply had to ask yourself, "Is this right or wrong?" After a Society Ending Event, the lines between right and wrong quickly become blurred. It will no longer be a simple right or wrong answer. You will be faced with decisions that involve your survival or that of a family member. It is amazing what you will do when the life of your spouse or child is at risk. One of the things that Nazi Germany excelled at was torture. They perfected the art. They learned early on that a naked man loses all arrogance. Moreover, the way to control a man was to threaten to sexually assault his wife. A man will lose all bravado when faced with compliance or watching his wife get assaulted. Along the same lines, the Nazis learned that the way to control a woman was to threaten the life of her child. In fact, while the Nazis separated men from women into two separate concentration camps, the children were kept at the same camp as the women.

I point this out to show you how far a person will go to insure the safety of those that they hold most precious. And to ask the question, how far are you willing to go to protect the ones you love? For most people reading this, the answer is simple. I would do anything to protect my family. The problem is that when they make that statement they are doing so with the thought that they live in the world of today, not after a Society Ending Event. I am willing to bet that at least 9 out of 10 people reading this immediately took the context of that question to mean "protect my family against physical injury". In the world following a Society Ending Event, it is not just about protecting them from physical injury. It is also about protecting them from disease, from thirst, and from starvation. What are you willing to do to insure that your children have enough to eat at night? How will you cope with the realization that you are watching your child starve to death? To add to this, how will you cope if you are watching your child starve to death as a result of your lack of preparedness prior to a Society Ending Event?

It is much easier to develop the Survival Mindset when times are normal than to attempt to adapt to it once the Schumer Hits the Fan. By mentally preparing now, you increase your chances of survival astronomically. There are many steps you can take to achieve this, and we will discuss them in the following paragraphs. But first, I have to ask one more time.

Do you still want to survive?

Facial Expression Recognition. Facial Expression Recognition is a great way to start developing the survival mindset. There are many books and videos on the subject. If this sounds like something that may be boring, start by watching a few episodes of "Lie to Me" on Netflix. This was a TV show wherein the main character, Dr. Liteman, was a body language expert that was used by several government agencies to help solve crimes. This show will help you to generate interest in Facial Expression Recognition. A good book on the subject is "Unmasking the Face" by Wallace Friesen. You can purchase it on Amazon.com for roughly $15.

The importance of Facial Expression Recognition is that once you have learned how to read a person's face, you will be able to read their thoughts and intentions. A side note is that it will also help you to understand when you have said something to your wife that upset her or when your children are lying to you. But for Developing the Survival Mindset, it is key so that you will know by a person's facial expression if their intention is to hurt you or your family. It takes the average human 1.8 seconds to make up their mind to discharge their weapon and hurt another human. It then takes another .9 seconds to complete the act. But knowing from their expressions when they make the decision to act, you can get the draw on them. Those .9 seconds could be the difference between life or death for you or a family member.

Body Language. By being able to pick up clues to a person's intentions by simply reading their body language, you can either de-escalate and issue, or help to bring it to fruition. A great book on body language is *"How to Read a Person Like a Book: Observing Body Language to Know What People Are Thinking"* by Gabriel Grayson. You can get a copy at Barnes and Noble for under $12.

Let me give you an example of body language. In 2010, I was involved in negotiating a contract for a $4.3 million project. When I entered the conference room for the negotiations, I was alone from my company, and the company I was trying to get the bid with had eleven employees in the conference. One of the hardest things to do when face with a major sales negotiation is to determine who the true decision maker in the room is. It is usually not the person doing the speaking for the other company. Prior to the meeting beginning, I spent some one on one time with the person that would be doing the bulk of the talking for the other company by the door to the meeting room. I noticed that the entire time we were talking he was standing with his arms folded, palms flat against his chest. When he uncrossed his arms, he clasped his hands together in front of his crotch area. Another thing I noticed was that while we were talking, he kept shifting around, but his feet always pointed toward the door. These things told me that he was intimidated by me, felt insecure in my presence, and would prefer to not be the one talking with me. How did I recognize this? The answer is simple. When a person points their feet toward the door this indicates a desire to leave, or flee. When someone does this when you are speaking with them it means they do not want to be speaking with you and are looking for a way to flee. Those of you reading this that have teenage children, this is a good sign to know when they are feeling guilty about something and are lying to you about it. When a person crosses their arms across their chest and in front of their crotch, it is a subconscious attempt to protect their vital areas. This signifies that they are feeling threatened. If it is someone you barely know, this indicates that they feel inferior to you. If it is someone you know well, it could indicate that they are feeling hurt by something you have said or done. Guys, when you come home and your wife is standing there with her arms crossed, palms inward, across her chest and has an angry look on her face, it is not anger. It is hurt or rejection. The easiest way to diffuse that situation is to sincerely tell her that you realize by her expression that she is hurt by something you have said or done and sincerely apologize for it. It is easier to diffuse her hurt feelings, then calmly discuss the issue, that to yell and scream for hours, further hurting her feelings, and never resolving the initial issue.

The point of all this is that the third stair to Developing the Survival Mindset is in understanding when a threat is present or not. After a Society Ending Event, it is of great importance that when you encounter a stranger, it is easy for you to quickly determine their intentions by their body language and facial expressions. When we live in a world of daily fear and struggle, we will do things that will reform our personalities. Every edge you can gain now, while the world seems whole, will help you then and strengthen your chances of surviving.

Coping with Lose. The hardest thing you will ever deal with is the death of a child. The second hardest will be the death of a spouse. The only thing that increases the difficulty of dealing with this grief is the knowledge that it was your actions or inactions that caused the death. You need to realize, now when the world is still whole, that after a Society Ending Event people are going to die. They will die from violence. They will die from accidents. They will die of thirst or starvation. They will die from exposure. Whatever the cause, people will die. Statistically, you will lose family members, friends, and loved ones. Accept it now, not later.
Grief can lead to depression and depression negatively affects your body physically. Following a Society Ending Event, people who are depressed

have less than a ten percent chance of survival. Depression will greatly reduce your chances of making it through the principal dying times. It will fatigue you. It will kill you. If you can bring yourself to accept that people you know are going to die, when it happens it will be easier to accept and cope with.

Force on Force Training. The more training you can do now, mentally and physically, the greater your chances of survival post event. The biggest misconception people have is that they feel that since they can shoot the center of a paper target at 20 yards with their pistols that they are ready to live in a world where a firearm is a necessity. I am fond of the saying "paper targets will not break into your house in the middle of the night". There are a plethora of firearms instructors in the country that perform Force on Force instruction. Using Simunition rounds to actually shoot at another person, creates a mindset of shooting at a person. This training WILL save your life if you are ever faced with a violent confrontation. Following WWII, our military leaders realized that less than nine percent of our infantrymen actually knowingly shot at the enemy with the intent to kill them. By Vietnam, the military stopped training with circular targets and started using silhouette targets. They found that the results were better. However, now they use simmunitions and have found the results to be tremendous. Studies show us that only one out of every one hundred people has the natural mental ability to shoot their firearm at another human, even in self defense. Worse yet is the realization that only one out of every one hundred of those people have the natural mental ability to discharge a weapon at another human knowing that it is going to take that person's life. That means that only one out of every ten thousand people carrying firearms for self defense has the natural mental ability to knowingly take another person's life. The rest of us will hesitate at the moment of truth, and that hesitation can get you killed or injured. The majority of us are civilized to the point where the ability to knowingly take a person's life has to be a learned ability, not a natural one. This is why I recommend Force on Force training as the final step to Developing the Survival Mindset.

Chapter Five

Morals of Survival

In a world gone crazy, morals that current exist will no longer apply. However, they will still exist. They need to exist. They must exist. The fact that the government and law enforcement will no longer be around is not an excuse to do what you want. That said, it is imperative that we maintain as many morals, as much civility, as is possible. This does not mean that you have to choose the high road as opposed to protecting yourself or your family. It does mean that your family is watching. And the world that will be born from the ashes of destruction is one that will be forged by our children. When we face a Society Ending Event, the future generations will conduct themselves using a code that is formed by the actions they watched us take and the moral standard we lived by.

Looting versus Salvaging. This is now and will continue to be a major moral issue. In the aftermath of a Society Ending Event, when the Rule of Law longer exists, what is the real difference between looting and salvaging? The answer is simple, even though the application is much more difficult.
Looting

From Wikipedia, the free encyclopedia

Looting also referred to as sacking, plundering, despoiling, despoliation, and pillaging—is the indiscriminate taking of goods by force as part of a military or political victory, or during a catastrophe, such as during war,[1] natural disaster,[2] or rioting.[3] The term is also used in a broader sense, to describe egregious instances of theft and embezzlement, such as the "plundering" of private or public assets by corrupt or greedy authorities.[4] Looting is loosely distinguished from scavenging by the objects taken; scavenging implies taking of essential items such as food, water, shelter, or other material needed for survival while looting implies items of luxury or not necessary for survival such as art work, precious metals or other valuables. The proceeds of all these activities can be described as loot, plunder, or pillage.

The main difference between looting and salvaging is that when you enter another person's home or business and take something from them by force or violence, this is looting and is morally wrong. However, if that home or business is abandoned, you have a moral obligation to your family to salvage the items you or they need to survive.

To Help or Not To Help. This is the second most important moral of survival. Read the following scenarios and ask yourself what is morally correct in each situation.

Situation One

On day 29 following a Society Ending Event, a group consisting of two men, three woman (one of them pregnant), and two small children approach you home or retreat. When they stop and ask you for food, what do you do? After all, your resources are limited. You realize that to give them enough food and water for one day will take two days food and water away from you and your family. To not help them will speed up their death. If you do help them, you run the risk of them realizing you have plenty of supplies and coming back after nightfall to take more from you by force. What do you do?

Situation Two

Your best friend for twenty years has always made fun of the fact that you were preparing for this very event. No matter what information you gave him he always responded with something stupid like, "This is the United States of America. Nothing is going to happen. You are just paranoid." He never prepared. Instead, he spent his money on making his house bigger or buying a new car or boat. You have watched his children grow up and love them as if they were your own. On Day Six following a Society Ending Event, he shows up at your house asking that you take him in. He has not brought any provisions with him and his family is hungry, tired, and in need of a bath. What do you do?

Situation Three

Day Seventeen following a Society Ending Even, a man shows up at your retreat with his wife and 16 year old daughter. He is pushing a wheelbarrow that contains all of their worldly belongings. When they stop at your front gate, he explains that he has a reloading machine and is willing to reload up to 1000 rounds of ammo in exchange a day's food, one night's shelter, and a shower for each one of them. What do you do?

Situation Four

At eleven thirty pm on the twenty eighth day following a Society Ending Event, you find a man sneaking into your garage carrying a pistol and a gas can. What do you do?

Situation Five

On the sixty third day following a Society Ending Event, your daughter falls off a ladder and breaks her leg. You try to set it, but by the third day you realize it is infected. There is a guy that you know of that lives a few streets over that was very much into preparation before the world ended. You know he has medical supplies, probably antibiotics. You go to his house and offer a really good trade, but he refuses to trade with you. What do you do?

Situation Six

By the end of the fourth month following a Society Ending Event, your supplies are starting to run low. Because you have a well on your property, you have plenty of water. But since you only started preparing a few months before the world ended, you are running out of food. You leave your house in search of some food and find a house that is obviously abandoned. Looking around inside the house, you find food, some silver, and some other items that could benefit your family. What do you do?

The previous situations may seem unlikely for the world as it exists today. I mean, this is the United States of America, right? Today, if you came across a family begging for food, you would give them some. If your friend lost everything, you would loan him some money. If a family offered to work for food, you would let them to help them out. If you saw a guy breaking into your garage, you would lock your house doors and call the police. If your daughter broke her arm, you would take her to the hospital. And if you ran out food, you would go to the store and buy some. After each of these situations, you would be able to sleep at night.

However, we are not talking about these situations in the world as it exists today but as it will exist after a Society Ending Event. So what is the correct response to each of these situations? This is where things get tricky. As you sit there in your comfortable home on your comfortable chair reading this book, things seems great. Moreover, you might not be able to picture yourself taking the actions I am about to describe. The cold hard reality is that in a world without government, rule of law, and critical services, you are on your own. In a post Society Ending Event world, the following responses to these situations may be morally questionable, but they are what they are.

Situation One

Following a Society Ending Event, resources will become very scarce immediately, and nonexistent within a matter of days. You will only have what you were able to get in the first twenty four hours following the event and what you were able to stockpile prior to the event. The parents should have taken every step to provide for their family before the world went to crap. However, in this situation they did not. So is it the kids fault? No. But yet, you cannot give to the kids without tipping off the adults that you have supplies. This is a tricky situation wherein each person that encounters this situation will have to make up their own mind as too how to proceed. As for me, I will explain to the adults that I have nothing to spare more than one day worth of food and water for each of them. Then I would explain that my community has housing and educational services for the children as well as doctors and a full security force. If they want to provide for their children, they can leave them with the community and know that they are taken care of and will survive. But we will not allow the adults to ever come back and will use whatever means necessary to insure they do not.

Situation Two

It is harsh, but is also the reality of the situation. I would give him one day's worth of food and water per family member then send them on their way. If they want to leave the kids, that would be fine.

Situation Three

This one is simple. No moral dilemma here at all. I would make the trade. Then, while they were resting and eating, I would have the members of my group interview them to see if they could be integrated into the community. The community cannot grow if we do not allow outsiders to join. This family did not come begging. They came and offered a valuable service that was worth more than what they were asking for. This shows a family of high standing and strong work and moral code.

Situation Four

Do I really need to spell out what I would do here? No questions asked, no warning given. In a world without rule of law, the law is what you are able to enforce with your own hand.

Situation Five

Hands down, no moral issue here. I would do what I had to do to keep my daughter safe. If the person is unwilling to trade for what my daughter needs to survive and he understands she will die without it, I will do what needs to be done to keep my daughter alive.

Situation Six

If the home is abandoned, there is nothing wrong with salvaging what you can use. Take what you need and only what you need. Remember that finding this abandoned treasure is a blessing. Only take what you need and leave the rest for the next person.

One of the biggest hindrances to surviving in a post Society Ending Event world is changing our mindset from what is right and wrong now to what will be right and wrong after the event. Any item that you discover that has been abandoned and is of use to you or your family is fair game. Take it and use it. But do not become a looter. Once you start down that path, there is no turning back. The opposite side of this whole looting versus salvaging excursion is that if you have to choose between looting and saving the life of a family member, you should choose their life over a strangers every time. Do not tolerate looters on your property. Today, we would call 911. After a Society Ending Event, there is no one to call and you must do what you must do. Last, do not be closed minded about helping others out. My wife and I have stockpiled one hundred one day ration packs. This is food and water for one person for one day. In the aftermath of a Society Ending Event, I will help as many people as I can, as long as they deserve the help and I can afford to do so. And yes, I am the one who will decide who is deserving and who is not deserving.

Today, we ask the following questions before taking action:

- **Is this action morally and ethically right?**
- **If I take this action, will anyone be hurt by my deeds?**

Following a Society Ending Event, the questions should be:

- **How will future generations look back upon this action?**
- **Is this how I want my children to remember this time in their lives?**
- **Will this action benefit my family?**
- **Will this action save a family members life?**
- **Who is more important, that stranger or my spouse or child?**

Chapter Six

Preparing for TEOTWAWKI

TEOTWAWKI stands for The End Of The World As We Know It. How do we prepare for that? Seriously, how can any one person prepare completely for the End of the World as We Know It? Many people who are new to the Self Reliant Lifestyle ask themselves this question every day. Every seminar I do, every group that I speak to, every training weekend we do, there is always at least one person who comes to me and tells me how overwhelmed they are. Recognizing just how fragile our world is can be very scary. Trying to prepare for the end of the world, is even scarier. Especially when you realize that the majority of people who become Self Reliant as adults have done so initially out of fear.

Fear can be a killer. It can paralyze us and force us to do things we never would have thought we could do. It can make us think we have gone off the deep end. On the other end of the spectrum, fear can be a great thing if we channel it correctly.

This chapter is written for those in the first two stages of getting prepared. If you follow these simple steps, it will alleviate much of the stress and anxiety most people experience in the first two stages of preparing.

The first step in preparing for TEOTWAWKI is recognizing the need to prepare as well what took place to get us to recognize that fact. If fear was the great motivator, then lets channel that and make the fear work for us. When I meet people new to the Self Reliant lifestyle who have fears and anxiety over getting prepared, the first thing I have them do is make a list of all the things they are fearful of. Then I challenge them to research those particular items. Once they have researched the things that make them afraid, I teach them to understand what they have researched. This allows me to begin to help them to get prepared. The main thing to remember here is that no matter what happens it is survivable. Societies have ended in the past. Some as a result to a failed economy, some through war and violence. Some have ended by floods and earthquakes. Some by meteors and asteroids. The key thing to remember and hold onto is that if any of those things were not survivable, the human race would not be here. You would not be reading this book. For that matter, I would not have been here to write it.

Everything we are currently going through; political events, man-made disasters, natural disasters, all these things are cyclic. The world has been here before and will be here again. Once you recognize that, you become aware of the fact that if others had survived it, you can too. So, let's get ready to survive.

Step one to getting prepared is to recognize what it is you are preparing for. Some people are preparing for an economic collapse. Others civil unrest or an EMP or a major quake. Personally, I am preparing for everything. I do not know what the future holds. What I do know is that a prudent man that loves his family does what he can to insure their safety and comfort. For me, that includes preparing for TEOTWAWKI. As such, I have prepared for, and continue to prepare for, any possible negative outcome. I believe that if you prepare for the worse and hope for the best, no matter the situation, you will survive. For me, preparing for TEOTWAWKI is equally as important as having insurance. I don't plan for my house to catch fire or to have a car accident, but I have insurance for both and have experienced both. Similarly, I don't want the world to end, but I have prepared for it.

Step two is recognizing the geographic and environment location that you live in. Research your area. Know what edible plants are indigenous to your surroundings. Know what plants grow, so you know what you need for your garden. Two key items you should have. The first is a Farmer's Almanac showing weather histories and patterns as well as growing cycles and seasons. This can be purchase at any chain book store such as Books A Million or Barnes and Noble. The second item is a city and state map. You should know your surrounding area. Most Chambers of Commerce will have maps available for the city and/or county at no charge. Most state visitor centers will have state maps for free. If these items won't cost you anything and can save your life, shouldn't you pick some up today. It would be a good idea to get multiple copies. Keep one ion your car, one in your Get Home bag, and one in your house. If you have supplies cached somewhere, you should have maps there as well.

Step three is to prepare a "Get Home Bag" or "Emergency Bag" for each vehicle and each family member. The key to a good bag is to make sure that the items you put into the bag are the items you would need to get home from wherever you may be, and can withstand fluctuating temperatures from below freezing up to three hundred degrees. Why so hot? Because during the summer time, the trunks of cars and inside of cars can see temperatures up to three hundred degrees. One of the worst things that can happen to you is encounter a catastrophic event that would cause you to have to rely on your Get Home Bag only to find out that the food and water inside have gone bad or the candles have melted all over the chem.-lights, etc. We will go into this more in another chapter. Suffice for now that you bag needs to have everything you would need to survive to get you home. The basic rule of thumb is one day supply for every 10 miles you have to walk. Remember, lighter is better.

Step four is to go through your house and make an inventory of all your consumables. This can be an overwhelming task, so take your time and go room to room. Go into the bathrooms and inventory what is there that you purchase on a regular basis. Then move to the laundry room, then the kitchen. While making this list, notate next to each item how often you have to buy it. For example, weekly, monthly, every other month, once a year, and so on. This will help you to make an inventory of what you will need for two years for your house. The goal is to build a two year supply, but also to do so by getting what you need at the same levels. For example, you do not want to have a two year supply of toilet paper, medical supplies, and shampoo, and not have any food or water. The simplest way to get what you need is to look at your two year list and divide it into twenty four months. Then, make twenty four copies of your monthly needs. Purchase an entire month and complete that month's checklist before you move on to the next month. This will insure that your preparations stay even and on track without getting too much of one item and not enough of another.

Step five is where it starts to get fun. Once you have your Get Home Bags and a two year supply of everything your family needs, you can start expanding your preparations. At this time, you can invest in solar ovens, solar water purifiers, solar generators, Kelley stoves, etc et al. Believe me, by the time you have acquired everything you need for two years, there will be a long list of items you will have seen and decided you had to have. The key is to make sure that you have your needs filled before you spend time and money on the wants.

Chapter Seven

Bug In or Bug Out

This is a long standing debate amongst those that practice the Self Reliant Lifestyle. When the SHTF, do you bug out or do you bug in? This is a choice you will have to make on your own. Personally, I believe in bugging in. Mainly because of the following two reasons:

- If you bug out and do not have a plan on where you are going or have supplies cached at that location, you will become a looter, become a refugee, or become a dead person. Those are the only three outcomes if you do not have a plan.
- If you do have a plan and a location, and cannot get there with the resources you have, you will become a looter, become a refugee, or become dead.

The best way to cope with the stress, anxiety, and depression that most people will experience following a Society Ending Event is to keep life a normal as possible. If your children are school age, they should do school work for several hours a day. If your regularly spend an hour reading your bible every day, you should continue to do so. When the world is falling apart around you, simple tasks that you performed when the world was whole can help you to maintain a permanent link with your sanity. So, with that said, I always prescribe bugging in. Similarly, I prescribe having a "Get Home Bag" as opposed to a "Bug Out Bag". While you may be asking what the difference is between the two, suffice to say that the contents of each are extremely different.

A Bug Out Bag, or BOB, is a bag that contains everything you would need to survive from the time you leave your home until the time you get to your destination. Since you will be carrying a lot of supplies on your back, and will want to carry as much as possible, you want lighter items that will be durable and hold up to stressful situations for extended amounts of time. It needs to contains items to protect and shelter you from weather. It needs to contain a large amount of food.

A Get Home Bag is completely different. This bag needs to contain everything you need to get you home should you be unable to drive there. A minor medical kit, extra socks and underwear, gloves are more important than a thirty day supply of long shelf life freeze dried food. At the end of this chapter, I have included a detailed list of what you need for your Get Home Bag and the trunk of your vehicle. The list is a generalized list of suggestions. You will need to modify it for your geographical location.

The key to your family's survival is to survive together. Statistics show that with an average family of four consisting of an adult male, adult female, and two children under the age of ten years old, the chances of survival for the children is in the eighty percentile and the mother in the ninety percentile. However, when you remove the father from the equation, the statistics show a major drop in the percentage of survivability for the wife and children. The mother's chances of survival drop down to the forty percentile while the children's chances of survival drop to the twenty percentile. If you remove both the father and the mother from the equation, the chances for the children drop to two percent. For these reasons, it is my belief that bugging in and staying together as a family leads to the strongest chance of a total family survival.

The worst possible thing that could happen during day one is for your family to be looking for you while you are looking for them, and you all miss each other. That is why I preach to everyone that will listen the need for having a Family Emergency Response Plan. A Family Emergency Response Plan should include the following:

- Each Get Home Bag should contain a map showing at least three routes, each highlighted in a different color. Along each route there should be check point locations. Each Get Home Bag Map should be identical to the others. This way, each person has a map showing their own likely routes as well as the routes of the other family members. Even when cell phone lines are congested, text messages will still get through. If the grid has gone down, most cell phones will still work for 48 hours because most of the cell phone towers have 48 hour battery backup systems. With each person having a map showing both their routes and the routes of the other family members, you can send a bulk text with the route color and last check point, such as Pink 3. This will allow the other family members to know your last known location.

- Have a response plan and make sure each family member knows there function within the plan. For example, if you have a spouse and two children in elementary school, the children should know that if they are at home and a disaster hits they need to go inside the house and lock the doors. If they are at school, they need to know to stay at school until one or both of their parents get there. If the mother works somewhere between the fathers work and the children's school, she needs to wait at work until the father gets there, then they need to proceed to the children's school. There is safety in numbers. A man and woman walking a long distance together have a greater chance of survival than either one of them will have individually.

Once you have both a Family Emergency Response Plan and maps to your home from work, school, the grandparents house, etc et al; you will need to drill the plan into each family members head. Make sure each person knows what they need to do as well as what everyone else will be doing. Knowledge of where your family is and what they are doing is key to your own survival while you are separated in the chaos. If you do not need to worry about them, then you can focus on your own survival until you can get to them.

Have a plan. Get a Get Home Bag. Practice your plan. Make sure everyone in your family knows your plan. If you work more than an hour from home, find a cache place somewhere along the route and stockpile some supplies at that locations. Make sure your family members know the location and the combination to the lock. Climate controlled storage rooms make great cache locations. They can also be a source of shelter for a few days if the need arises. I always recommend to families with college age kids to find a storage unit close to campus and cache some supplies there as well as extra gas. When the SHTF, the kids can stay in the storage unit with food, water, fire, and shelter until their parents can get there to get them.

Recommended List of Items for a Get Home Bag

Quantity   Person 1

Standard Kit

1	Non Descript Bag
4	Underwear
4	Socks
4	T Shirts
1	Sweatshirt
1	Pair Jeans
1	Good Set of Hiking Boots
1	Foot Powder
2	Tooth Brush
1	Tooth Paste
1	Deodorant
1	Comb or Brush
1	Small Mirror
1	Flashlight with Red Lenses Option
4	Flashlight Batteries
1	Quality Fixed Blade Knife
1	Compass
2	Map of Area
1	Lock Pick Set
1	Pry Bar
1	Small Tent
1	Emergency Sleeping Bag
1	Emergency Blanket
1	Small Bottle with Eye Dropper filled with generic bleach (3 oz.)
50	Cotton Balls in a zip lock bag
5	Gallon Size Zip Lock Bags

30 Storm Proof Matches
1 Utility Gloves
5 Latex Gloves
1 25 oz. Water Bottle
1 Poncho
1 Small Camp Stove
1 Canteen Cup
1 Plastic Canteen
1 Canteen Cover
3 Hexa Pots
6 Insta Fire
3 Medical Mask
5 6 Hour Chem Lights
2 Day worth of rations standard
  Day worth of rations for every 10 miles
1 from home.

Standard Trauma Kit

1 4.0 Silk Sutures
1 6.0 Silk Sutures
1 Small Surgical Kit
4 Latex Gloves
3 2" Gauze
3 4" Gauze
3 6" Gauze
12 Small Band-Aids
12 Large Band-Aids
1 Ace Bandage
1 Sling
2 Pressure Bandage
1 Quick Clot Gauze

12	Alcohol Wipes
1	Batadine
1	Petroleum Jelly
4	Medical Super Glue
12	Ibuprofen
12	Aspirin
12	Vitamin C Tablets
12	Vitamin B Tablets
1	Tweezers
1	Neosporin

Chapter Eight

Two is One/ One is None

I have always believed that there is strength in numbers. In a post Society Ending Event, trying to survive on your own and away from home is pretty much the same as committing suicide. Everyone has to sleep at some point. If you are hurt or injured, having someone with you is the surest way to insure your own survival. I am convinced, that if my wife and I are together, our chances of survival is triple what they would be if we are on our own. For those who think they are better off alone, I ask you the following questions:

- Who will stand guard over you while you sleep?
- Who will set your broken bone or suture your deep wound?
- Who will help you over a two person obstacle?

I am constantly being asked "How do I increase my chances of survival if I am forced to bug out?" My answer is always the same. There is strength in numbers. There are too many things that can go wrong in a post Society Ending Event world. If you are forced to bug out, remember that the bigger your group is, the stronger it is.

For me, there is no one I trust more than my wife. We both know each other's strengths and weaknesses. I know that when I am sleeping she will be awake and watchful. I know that if I am hurt or injured, she will provide the medical attention I need until I recover. I know that she will always put my life before hers, as she knows I will put her life before my own. We both know that we have a greater chance of making it home together than we do apart. We know that our daughter's survival is directly dependent on our ability to get to her and, as a unit, move to our house.

The main thing to remember here, is that my wife and I trust each other completely. For purely selfish reasons (our own survival) we have to be completely unselfish and put the other's need and survival before our own. In my seminars I often joke that I would hate to be the man who is forced to rely on my wife to cover my back in a survival situation if I had spent years mentally and physically abusing her. Think about it. Would you feel safe having a woman watch your back with a loaded firearm in a world without rule of law that you had abused? I sure wouldn't. With that said, the trust that comes with you being able to depend on your spouse with your life starts now, not after the world ends. Become unselfish. Put their needs above your own. Around the fifteen year mark of our marriage, I learned a very valuable lesson. I learned that if I put her needs above my own, and took care of her needs one hundred percent, what would she have to do with her time? The answer was simple. She would have the time and energy to take care of all of my needs.

Perception IS Reality. This started with simple selfishness. I had recently discovered that when I would get frustrated or angry with her for wanting to discuss something with me while I was watching TV that it would end in an argument that would last longer than the conversation would have to begin with. Instead of missing 10 minutes of the game by talking with her, I would miss forty minutes of the game by arguing with her. So one day she came into the room and asked if she could talk to me about something. Instead of getting frustrated by trying to have a conversation with her and watching the game, I turned the TV off and turned my attention toward her. Needless to say, this shocked her. Her perception of my actions was that whatever she had to say to me was more important to me than the game I was watching on TV. This made her feel good about herself and our relationship. The reality for me was that I just wanted to get the conversation over with to get back to my game. I learned two lessons that night. The first was that you get back to the TV show quicker if you devote all of your attention to the conversation. The second was that when your wife believes she is more important to you than a TV show, she is secure in your marriage and will wait until the next commercial before asking you a question. From there, I learned that the more I focused on her needs, there more she focused on my needs.

I have tried, over the last eight years, to apply this ideology every aspect of our marriage and have found that by being completely unselfish, I get everything I want, and so does she. The arguments have ended, and we now view the other as being not just our spouse but also our best friend. Why is this important? Because when the SHTF, you will want a spouse who will stand beside you. Two is one. One is none.

Chapter Nine

Fortifying Your Home

Every time I do a seminar or public speaking engagement, I am asked the same question time and again. *"How do I fortify my home against invaders after a Society Ending Event?"* The answer is always the same, you don't.

The saying "The best offense is a great defense" holds true with any situation, not just sports. When my daughter was playing travel soccer, the coach informed us that she was a great forward, but she was also a natural goal keeper and with some training could be one of the best in the state. So we sat her down that evening and explained her options. When she complained about being a keeper instead of a forward I explained to her that it took ten players to score a goal, but only one person controlled the goal. She then countered that the ball had to get through ten players to reach the goal. Admitting she was correct, I informed her that the keeper was always the one credited with the save. While offensive players determined who won the game, the keeper determined who would lose.

The point of this story is that perception is reality. Many people believe that they will have to defend their home and supplies against attacks from looters. They think this because they are thinking offensively. My belief is to think defensively. Instead of focusing your efforts on how to fortify your home from attack, think defensively on how to fortify your home by making it appear to have already been looted. In other words, make your home look as if it is not worth defending.

The important thing to consider here is that the first thirty days following a Society Ending Event will be the time of exodus from the major cities. Anyone who is able to leave will leave. People will leave in a hurry, thereby turning the neighborhoods and streets into a chaotic, impassable mess. The key to fortifying your home is to embrace the chaos. Remember chaos theory from chapter one? *You have to stare into the chaos and focus to see the beauty in the patterns as they develop.* The average looter does not take the time to do so. They respond to the chaos by searching for the non-chaotic. In other words, when all the homes in a neighborhood look disheveled and abandoned, the homes that still look normal will stick out amongst the chaos. These are the homes that the looters will focus their attention on.

Think like a looter for a moment. You have not eaten in two days; you are hungry, tired, and desperate. Because you were not self reliant prior to the Society Ending Event, you are ill prepared. When the event took place, you waited for the first eight days at home expecting things to return to normal. During those eight days, you ate all your food and did not think to conserve water until the water stopped running. On day nine you left your home in search of food. Prior to leaving, you dug your dad's old pistol out from under the bed only to realize that it only had 16 bullets with it. Here you are on day sixteen. No food or water, and down to your last three bullets. You are tired and you are hungry. You enter a neighborhood that is chaotic with abandoned clothing, furniture, and electronics. Cars have windows broke out and the doors are open. You notice that three houses look as if they had been on fire recently. There is a dead person lying in the road. Another sitting behind the wheel of a car, door open, and a bullet hole in her head. Amidst all the chaos, you see one home that does not look like it has been looted. There are no cars in the driveway, and you notice smoke coming from a smoke stack on the roof. You see that the curtains are drawn shut. From your location, you can hear the dull hum of a motor. At first, you think it is a car in the garage until, getting closer to the house, you realize it is a generator. Thinking at first that the residents might be inclined to help you, maybe give you some food and water, you knock on the front door. You hear a dog barking and notice that someone has turned off the generator, but no one has come to the door. This frustrates you and you bang harder. Still no one answers the door. Finally, after a few minutes of banging with no answer, you realize other people have come to see what you have found. You explain what has happened and that no one will answer the door to give you any food. Quickly, you are joined by several others; people who are hungry and desperate like yourself. Soon, a crowd of people have surrounded the house and are looking for ways to get inside. Eventually, someone breaks a window and people start to enter the house only to be met with gun fire. The people inside are about to have a bad day.

The single most important piece of advice I can give someone who will be bugging in and lives near a major city is embrace the chaos. Your goal is to not have to defend your house when the looters come. Let the looters go to your neighbor's house. When a looter enters your neighborhood, and sees your house, they should realize that there is nothing to gain by going into your house. You have to change the perceptions of the looters by making your house look like it is already abandoned and looted and that by entering your home, death will follow. You have to make your home look as if entering the home will cost a looter more than anything that could be left in the home. This creates the reality for the looter that your home is not worth messing with. Here are some tips to help you accomplish this goal.

Tip Number One. Every emergency bug in kit should contain a quarantine label. Notice I say label and not a sign. This should be a full page label that can quickly be attached to a door or window. You can go online and find several available for download or you can make your own. Once you find the one you want, have your local print shop print it out for you. Make it look realistic, so try to avoid the "zombie" ones most people are found of buying. Remember, this is not a cool sign to hang in your bedroom. This is a tool that can help save your life. One of the cheapest tools to purchase that will help you survive.

Tip Number Two. When boarding up your house, your goal is to board up the outside, not the inside. During the first few days of the Society Ending Event, those in power will hold onto the belief that things will return to normal, therefore they will attempt to maintain order. For the first two weeks, any home that is forcibly evacuated will be done so very quickly. Meaning that the boards over the doors and windows will not be neat and orderly, but instead be uneven and using as few boards as possible. If you are trying to make your house look as if there is nothing of value inside, you will board up the doors and windows from the outside to make it look as if it was done by someone who was in a hurry. For some good examples, do a Google search of homes in the aftermath of Hurricane's Katrina and Sandy. After you have boarded up the outside, put some quarantine signs over the boards and draw some markings on the quarantine labels. Do a Google search for "Katrina Crosses" for an example of what the symbols need to look like.

Tip Number Three. Your emergency bug in kit should contain black sheets; one for each window. On the inside of your home, closes your curtains, then cover them with the black sheets. This will ensure that no light is visible from the outside of your home. For additional protection from entry, once you have hung the black sheets, nail plywood over the windows from the inside. This way, if someone tries to look through the wood planks covering the outside of the window, they will not be able to see anything inside the house.

Tip Number Four. For a generator, spend the extra money on a solar generator. There is a company in O'Fallon, Missouri named H2O Kinetics. They have some pretty great solar generators at very reasonable prices. The beauty of these generators is that you can mount the panel on your roof and have a renewable source of electricity that makes zero noise. You do not have to worry about noise or exhaust with a solar generator.

If you cannot afford a solar generator and choose instead to use a gas powered generator, you have to make it noise less. You also have to figure out a way to dampen the exhaust so that there is little fumes outside your house and zero fumes inside your house. The sound muffling is simple. Whatever room you have the generator in should have the walls, ceiling, and floor covered in foam. The cheapest form of sound baffling is egg shell mattresses found at Wal-Mart. Be sure to cover the floor also to help minimize the vibrations. Vibrations on a wood floor, even one with carpet, make noise. Vibrations on a concrete slab can be felt throughout the slab. If your generator is in your garage, and is sitting on the concrete, the vibrations can be felt in the driveway.

To exhaust the fumes, make sure to use a series of dryer vent and have it eventually leave the house. Install a filter at each junction with a minimum of three junctions to trap, or filter, the fumes. This way, if someone makes their way to the back of your house and stands next to the exhaust vent, it will minimize the odor of the fumes.

Tip Number Four. If the Society Ending Event is one that has rendered your vehicle inoperable such as an EMP or CME, or if the exodus has left the roads impassable to the point that your vehicle is no longer of use, use the vehicle as a deterrent as opposed to trying to keep it.

First, strip the car of anything that is of value. Using some duct tape, you can turn the front seat covers into a back pack using the seat belt for straps. The back seat cover can be turned into a sleeping bag or poncho using some duct tape. Small pieces of spare tire can be used as fire starters as they will light when wet and burn for long periods of time. Radio and speaker wires can be used as rope. The battery can be used for many things and should be removed.

The spare tire and tire iron should be kept as well. Remove any important documents from the glove box. Once you have removed all these items and put them inside your house, make the car look as if it was vandalized. Shatter the windows in the passenger and driver front doors. Leave the truck open. Make it look as valueless as possible. Last, using a screw driver, puncture a hole in the gas tank and collect the gas in glass jars for later use.

Once the car is left looking destroyed, a final precaution would be to spray some blood all over the interior on the driver side. This does not need to be your blood. You can use the blood of a chicken or rabbit if you raise them, or the first animal you kill if you are a hunter. The purpose of this is psychological. People try to avoid areas where other people have died. Some blood on the front seat of your car and on your front porch will spook many looters and make them move on to the next house.

A side note here is that if you are trapped away from home when the Society Ending Event takes place, all the items you can salvage from your car will help you survive. You can break a piece of glass into a knife and wrap the handle with duct tape. You can also use the tire iron for a weapon. When that is all you have, it can be pretty useful.

Tip Number Five. Make your house look as if it has already caught fire. A burned out house contains nothing of value to a looter. Your emergency bug in kit should contain a small hand torch. These can be purchased for less than thirty dollars at most major hardware stores. While you are there, buy some black spray paint. Once the Society Ending Event happens, use the torch to lightly burn and warp the siding at your gable vents. You want to use enough to warp the siding without risking setting the wood behind the siding on fire. Once this is done, enhance the burn look at the gable vents with the black spray paint. This is something that will be noticeable from a distance and might persuade looters from even approaching your house.

Tip Number Six. Anything inside the home that is no longer of value to you should be thrown about the front and back yards. For example, following an EMP or CME, your televisions, blue ray disk players, stereos, blenders, microwaves, etc. will no longer be of value to you. These, along with bags of trash and clothes you will no longer use, should be scattered around your porch, driveway, and yard to look as if people dropped them in a hurry. If you have extra blankets, scatter those as well.

Tip Number Seven. Entering your yard should be as painful to looters as possible. This is easily accomplished with the help of a fifty pound box of loose roofing nails from any major hardware store. Like sowing seed in a field, simply spread the nails all over the yards. Make walking, kneeling, or lying down in your yard very difficult. This could also act as an early warning system for when people are trying to sneak up on your house at night. Believe me, when someone kneels or steps on a two inch roofing nails, you will know it. There are other items you can use for this such as broken glass and thumb tacks. Use your imagination and get creative. The point is to put up as many obstacles as possible without making it look like you have done so.

Tip Number Eight. Remember that all plans can change at a moment's notice and are subject to the will of the enemy. This means that even if you do everything we have mentioned in the chapter, there might still be people who are desperate enough to try to get into your house. This is why I always recommend that you do not store your supplies in your garage or house unless you have no other option. The ideal place to hide your supplies is in the crawlspace of your home. By cutting a trap door in the floor of your closet, you can gain access to the crawlspace and be able to hide things such as buckets of food and ammo cans down there. This will also be one of the coolest places in your home. The additional advantage to having this is that you can use it as an escape hatch if your home is breached by looters without having to expose yourself to them. If you do not have a crawlspace, there are other ways of hiding your supplies in plain sight. For example, you could store your supplies in big dark plastic bens, and then write some on the side life Christmas Ornaments or Winter Clothes, etc. The key here is to stack the bens up with the top one actually containing what is written on the outside. You can also disguise your five gallon buckets with labels from paint cans. You can either buy the labels at paints stores or print them yourself. Again, make sure the top bucket actually contains paint.

These are just a few of the ways you can fortify your home for a bug in situation. Obviously, this is not an all inclusive list. Take these tips and use them as a starting point. Get creative. The idea here is to make the home look as if it has already been plundered and/or burned. The home has nothing of value inside. That death waits all who enter.

As I close this chapter, I am reminded of the story of Robin Hood. Specifically, those of Sherwood Forrest. As the story goes, Robin Hood and his Merry Men hung skeletons along the edge of Sherwood Forrest to create the illusion that *all who enter will greet death.* The more your home creates this perception, the less chance you have of someone actually trying to enter.

I was walking a friend's property giving him ideas on how to dissuade looters from coming onto his property after a Society Ending Event. He lives at the end of a long road, and as we stood at the entrance of his driveway, I told him this would be a great place to put an old car. I said that once the SHTF and it is clear that we have faced a Society Ending Event, he should put the old car there and shoot it full of holes. Then, the first time he slaughtered a chicken, he should spray the blood all over the inside of the car. This would create the illusion that someone tried to enter his property and died as a result. To further enhance the perception that no one should enter, is the fact that there is no grave and no body. Implying that the person who was killed at the scene was removed for dinner.

I want to leave you with this thought for those that live on large properties. Walk your property looking for all avenues of egress and digress. Look for areas where you could set up booby traps and get them ready. When we face the Society Ending Event, you do not want to waste time trying to get these things figured out. You should take the time now when the world is still whole to prepare for these things. Make a drawing of your property. Mark where you will put booby traps. You should also mark routes to escape in the event you are overrun. Somewhere along those routes, or at your evacuation location, have a cache of supplies buried that will last you twenty to thirty days. In these ways, you can slow down the advance of the looters and be able to evacuate in the event you cannot stop them. The nice thing about looters is that once they are done with the raping, pillaging, and burning, they will often move on. Remember the old saying, *"Survive to fight another day"*? This should be your motto when an overwhelming force attacks your retreat. By knowing where to go, and have supplies prepositioned, you insure that you will survive to fight another day.

Chapter Ten

Building Your Group

Putting together a group to help you and your family survive a Society Ending Event is not a simple thing to do. There is more involved than simply telling a bunch of people that they can come over when the SHTF and you will be the leader. If this is your plan for surviving a Society Ending Event, then do yourself a favor and give up now. Sell all your supplies, and take a vacation. There is a lot involved in building a future community. This chapter will discuss some of the ideas that you could use to build your community, or group as many of us like to say.

First, you need to organize your own thoughts as to what you hope the group will look like. Are you looking for a pacifist commune style group that will not last the first thirty seconds when attacked by a group of looters or do you want to have a group that will help shape the future of our country? I am sure that if you envisioned having a group that is pacifist, you would not be reading this book. So let's look at the second option.

The key is to remember that once the United States of America faces a Society Ending Event, it will never be the same again. There is a reason for calling it a Society Ending Event. At best, what is now the United States will be a series of smaller countries; as few as 7 and as many as a few hundred. One hundred years after a Society Ending Event, the history books will not be talking about our forefathers. They will not mention Washington, Jefferson, or Adams. They definitely will not mention Reagan, JFK, or Obama. A hundred years after a Society Ending Event the history books will talk about those few individuals who helped a small group survive the Chaos Years and forged a new nation. If you want your group to be mentioned in the history books, if you want to be one of those future forefathers, then first you must survive.

Dictatorship. The Democratic Experiment was not born of freedom, but of oppression. Independence was declared in 1776, the Constitution written in the 1780, and the Bill of Rights after that. The purpose of the War of Independence was to free the colonists from British Oppression. Meaning that at the time of the war, the colonists were oppressed. The freedoms that we have in the United States today were not immediate freedoms upon the colonists following the war. They are freedoms that gradually became a life style. The point, though, is that the reason the Democratic Experiment survived those first chaotic years was that the people were used to being oppressed. So, to get through the chaos years, the people were used to strict laws. I say this to point out that immediately following a Society Ending

Event, your group will require a leader whose word is absolute. During the Chaos Years, people will have to follow orders. Once things start to calm down, you can return to a Democratic Society, but in the beginning you will need to have a Dictatorship. Without a person in charge, everyone is doomed. The only chance of survival is for a fair but firm leader. One cautionary piece of advice; if you are not a good leader let someone else lead. Your life may very well depend on being in a group with a good leader. Do not let ego get in the way of survival.

Board of Elders. One person cannot possibly do everything. Remember chapter eight? Two is One and One is None? This needs to be your motto. Look at the core members of your group and assign them tasks as if they were a Board of Elders. Assign the tasks based, not on relationship, on personal experience and qualities. For example, why would you put your brother, who has zero military experience, in charge of external security when you have several members of your group who were Special Forces and have combat experience? Why would you put your wife in charge of food storage when you have a group member with twenty years experience running a major restaurant? The answer is that you wouldn't. The point is to allocate tasks to your core members based on experience and have them help you to set up the ground work for your group. Later in the chapter, we will discuss creating a Constitution for your group. This should not be written solely by you. You will need help. But establishing your core group member tasks before writing your Constitution, you will be able to rely on them for help writing it. This will also have the added benefit of drawing your core members into a tighter, more cohesive, unit. Below are some areas that you should look at while forming your group. These are key areas to building a community and should fall under the core member tasks. This, like previous lists, is not all inclusive. Use this as a starting point, and then customize it for your specific group needs. In smaller groups, members will have to have two jobs. One from the list below, and one that pertains more toward their specialty. When building a group, these positions are what you should be looking to implement first. By using core members to be the leaders in these tasks, you can give them the opportunity to write the rules and requirements for their departments. Additionally, the heads of each department should hold a seat on the Board of Elders.

Internal Security

This is basically like a police department. The Internal Security force is responsible for maintaining the rules of the group and enforcing the punishments as laid out in the Constitution. This group is responsible for perimeter security and group law enforcement. If you have a member of your group with Law Enforcement experience, they would be the prime candidate to head this department. If not, look to someone that has military experience. Try to avoid anyone that has a large ego and is looking out more for their own title than for the good of the community.

External Security

This is your military force. This department is responsible for deploying a Rapid Response Offensive should the group come under attack. Their secondary function is in leaving the secure area for missions such as salvage parties, hunting, insuring the neighbors are safe, and making contact with other groups who may be operating in your groups AO (Area of Operations). The leader of this department should have some combat leadership experience.

Logistics

Logistics is more than just knowing how much beans and bullets your group has on hand. The Logistics department is in charge of knowing what is readily on hand, what will be available for harvest and when, and what the group needs. This department is also in charge of making sure that all other departments have what they need and anticipates what other departments will need.

Critical Services

This is the catch all department. The Department Head for Critical Services will be over the Doctors, Teachers, and Maintenance Staff. Under their leadership will be anyone from the guy that cuts all the wood, to the Doctor, to the person in charge of reloading. The head of this department should be someone with experience in managing large groups of multi talented people.

These four department heads should be the Board of Elders for your community. Once you have outlined the basic vision for your group and brought these people onboard, you should let them take the outline of your vision and work through the creation of their departments. This will accomplish two goals; taking some of the pressure off you and building group cohesion.

The final role of the Board of Elders is to act as the Judiciary Branch of your Government. While you will need to maintain absolute rule, you need to remember that the members of your group are accustomed to living in a Democratic Society and you need to hold on to as much of that as possible. Therefore, when a group member has a complaint, they can take it to their specific department head, or Elder. If the Elder cannot resolve the complaint, they can bring it to the Group Leader. If a refugee is recommended for membership, the recommendation should be voted on by the Board of Elders. This will prevent the group members from looking negatively on the leader when a membership request is denied. The final role of the Board of Elders is to sit as jury over disputed, both civil and criminal. In this manner, again, the leader is not blamed but the whole group.

Constitution. Many people ask me how to write their Group Constitution. I normally jokingly say to take the United States Constitution with its Bill of Rights and all Amendments and start from there. And really, it is that simple. Maybe not the exact words, but the intent. Look at your group. Look at your core members. Look at your area of operations. Then, customize a Constitution to fit the needs of your group. I cannot tell you what your group needs. What I can tell you, however, is that now is the time to create your Constitution. Before we face a Society Ending Event you should lay out what the roles of each department are; what crimes will not be tolerated, the processes are for membership, and what the punishments are for violations of the rules.

For example, in our group, we have laid out certain crimes that will not be tolerated and what their punishments are. If a member is found guilty of committing murder, they are put to death. A person that is willing to commit murder is also a person who, if banished, will join with another group and disclose to them sensitive information about your group. We will banish any member that steals from another member. Additionally, any member who is found guilty a third time for falling asleep at their post will be banished. The problem with banishment in the aftermath of a Society Ending Event, banishment could mean death. Also, banishment is counter-productive to the concept of building the group.

New Memberships. The intent of any group is always the prosperity and growth of the group. To become bigger and stronger. In a world with the Rule of Law, there is strength in numbers. All groups should be open to new members; both pre and post Society Ending Event. Each group is different, and must be able to be in agreement with each other in regards to how new members may join the group. Something to keep in mind when determining who can or cannot join the group is to set up guidelines. You should do this now, when things are good, so that you may readily implement them when the Society Ending Event takes place.

In our group, a new member must be sponsored by an existing member. They must be voted on by all members of the group and receive a clear majority to attain membership. Once they have been approved as members, we require them to have a minimum of six month's supply of food and other consumables for each of their family members. Depending on which department they are assigned, they will be required to have additional items specific to their expertise. For example, doctors must have enough standard consumable medical supplies to treat minor injuries for forty five people for six months. Teachers are required to have school books for their age group specialty. Internal and External Security Members are required to have standardized equipment. We encourage each member to preposition their supplies, but it is not required.

Post Society Ending event Memberships are completely different. We all know that friends, neighbors, and family members of members are going to show up. Therefore, we have laid out a set of guidelines for new membership after a Society Ending Event. They are listed below.

- All new members must be sponsored by a current member.
- A member can only sponsor one person at a time.
- All people sponsored for membership will become Probationary Members for a term of thirty days.
- After the thirty day probationary time, all applicants for membership must appear before the Board of Elders for final approval.
- In the event of a tie among the Board of Elders, the Group Leader will cast the defining vote for membership.
- If an Elder is the sponsor of an applicant for membership, they Elder will not be eligible to cast a vote.

Voting Within the Group. Each group is different. You will have to customize your own rules and regulations. As concerns the ability to vote, here are some ideas from our group.

- A member family is entitled to one vote.
- A single member is entitled to one vote.

- All non members and probationary members are excluded from the right to vote.

A very wise man once told me that the time to lay out a partnership agreement is when all parties concerned want to form a partnership, not when they want to dissolve one. When I formed our group, I had the belief that the wisest course of action was to put everything in writing in the beginning, so that went the world went crazy, we would have guidelines in place to help us through the Chaos Times.

Proper Planning Prevents Poor Performance. If you did not already live the Self Reliant Lifestyle, or in the very least feel the need to start living it, you would not be reading this book. If you are living the Self Reliant Lifestyle, then you are already aware of the need to prepare. Look at writing your groups Constitution and forming your group as an extension of your preparations.

Chapter Eleven

Comprehensive List of Items

The below list is just another set of guidelines for you. Each person should customize their own list to meet their own needs and the needs of their families. I hope this list is helpful to you as you develop the Self Reliant Lifestyle.

This list is predicated on a one year supply of everything you need. The first person in your family obviously needs items that the second person does not.

One Year List of Supplies for One Person

Quantity	Person 1
	Basic Bug In Kit
	Clothing
2	Boots
2	Coats
2	Ear Muffs
2	Full Face Mask
2	Gloves
1	Goggles
2	Hats
1	Knit Cap

2	Long Johns
4	Pants
1	Parka Pants
2	Poncho
1	Poncho Liner
1	Rain Suit
1	Rubber boots
2	Scarf
2	Shoes
12	Socks Standard
1	Tactical Vest
6	Towels
12	T-shirts
12	Underwear
6	Wool Socks

Equipment

1	#10 Meat Grinder
	Adaptor –Propane Large to Small
1	can
12	Aluminum foil
4	Ant Flea & Tick killer
	Backpack Stove Fuel
2	Butane/Propane
6	Batteries 9 Volt 2 Pack
10	Batteries AA 6 Pack
10	Batteries AAA 8 Pack
10	Batteries C 6 Pack
10	Batteries D 6 Pack
2	Battery chargers
1	Binoculars
3	Blanket Twin/Full

6	Bleach
1	Bottle Opener
2	Bowl - Plastic- Cereal
4	Bucket 5 Gallon
12	Bunge Cord
2	Camp Chairs
12	Camp Fuel
1	Camp table
2	Can opener
48	Candles
2	Carbon Monoxide/Smoke Alarm
1	Cast Iron - Griddle
1	Cast Iron - Large Pan
6	Charcoal Bag Raw
4	Charcoal Lighter Fluid
60	Clothes Pins
2	Clothesline 100'
2	Coleman Hot Shower
24	Coleman Lantern Mantles #21
	Coleman's pump repair kit
1	Lantern/Stove
1	Compass
1	Cook Set 12pc
1	Cooking Thermometer
12	Copper Mesh Scourer Pads
1	Cork Screw
400	Cups Plastic or Styrofoam
2	Dish Washing Brush
12	Disposable Lighter
2	Disposable Lighter - Long
6	Duct Tape - Green
6	Duct Tape - Black

1	Dutch Oven
1	Dutch Oven Lifter
1	Edible Plant Book
3	Fire extinguisher
2	Fishing Pole
1	Fishing Tackle Kit
2	Flashlight - Crank Up
4	Flashlight - Battery Operated
1	12 Piece Kitchen Knife Set w/ Sharpener
1	Funnel
3	Garbage Cans
12	Gas Cans
4	Gloves - All Purpose
1	GPS
1	Grill Gas AND Charcoal Combo
1	Grommet Repair Kit
1	Hair Scissors
1	Hand Bow Saw
4	Hand Warmer Heat Packs 10 hour
20	Hexa Pots
1	Ice Chest – Keep things from freeze
2	Iodine Tablets Bottle
1	Kettle – Large Pot w/Lid
2	Lamp Oil
24	Lamp Wicks
2	Lantern - Propanc
2	Lantern Striker Lighter
24	Chem Light Sticks
2	Lighter –Butane- Refillable
4	Lighter Fluid – Butane Fuel
3	Maglite 3Watt LED 4Cell Bulb

1	Magnesium
1	Map City and County
1	Map Surrounding Cities and Counties
1	State Map
200	Waterproof Matches Package of 10
5	Standard Matches Box 200
1	Measuring Cups Set
1	Measuring Spoons Set
1	Meat Thermometer
6	Mouse Trap
2	Paper - 500 Sheet Package
400	Paper Plates
6	Paraffin Wax
24	Pen
24	Pencils
2	Pillows
4	Plastic Sheeting Visqueen 3.5 MIL 10'x25'
2	Plastic Sheeting Visqueen 4 MIL 3'x50'
12	Plastic Wrap
2	Playing Cards
1	Pocket Chainsaw
1	Pots & Pans Set
6	Propane – 5 gal
12	Propane Bottles– Camp Size
4	Rope 3/4" (100 feet)
3	Rubber bands (100 Count)
1	Safety Pins Box
2	Salt / Pepper Shaker
1	Scissors

4	Scotch-Brite Sponge
1	Sewing Kit
12	Sewing Needles
400	Plastic Forks
400	Plastic Knives
400	Plastic Spoons
1	Sling Shot
1	Solar Calculator
1	Solar Panel 12V
1	Solar Panel Invertors Kit
1	Spatula
2	Sta-Bil
1	Stainless Steel Bowl 3 QT
1	Stainless Steel Bowl 5 QT
	Stainless Steel Mixing Bowl -
1	Medium
1	Stove- Dual Fuel
12	Tarp Clip
6	Tarps (8'x10')
1	Tent
24	Tent Pegs
1	Tent Repair Kit
1	Thermometer 0-220 F
4	Tow Strap
6	Trash Bags – Black 2 Mil 45 Gallon
6	Trash Bags – Black 3 Mil
4	Water Bladder 5 gal E or F
1	Water Bladder Clean kit
2	Water Purification Tablets Bottle
1	Water Purifier
	Water Purifier Ceramic Filter
4	Element

3	WD40
12	Ziploc Bags- Gallon Box
12	Ziploc Bags- Quart Box
2	Zippo Lighter
4	Zippo Lighter Fluid - Ronsonol
2	Zippo Wick
1	Rifle
1000	Rifle Ammo
1	Shotgun
500	Shotgun Ammo
1	Pistol
1000	Pistol Ammo
1	Tactical Knife Dual Purpose
1	Rifle Spare Parts Kit
1	Shotgun Parts Kit
1	Pistol Parts Kit
4	55 Gallon Plastic Water Barrels
4	Water Tap for Plastic Barrel
	White Harvest Seed Heirloom Seed
2	Vault 30 Pouch Basic Kit

Hygiene

2	Chlorinating Sanitizer
1	Cocoa Butter Crème
12	Deodorant Anti-Perspirant
1	Finger Nail / Toe Nail Clippers
1	Finger Nail File
3	Floss Picks Package
2	Hair Brush
4	Hair Conditioner
9	Hair Shampoo
12	Hand Sanitizer

3 Insect Repellant 100% Deet
6 Insect Repellant Wipes
4 Lip Balm Chap Stick
12 Liquid Anti-Bacterial Soap
1 Medicated Body Powder
1 Mirror
2 Petroleum Jelly
Prescription Medicines (30 Day
12 Supply)
4 Q-Tips 250 Count Box
24 Shaving Razors
2 Skin So Soft
24 Soap - Bars
4 Soap Dish Washing
2 Sun Block 50
96 Toilet Paper
2 Tooth Brush
1 Tooth Brush - Holder
12 Tooth Paste
12 Towelette Package Moist
12 Shower Wipes Package
4 Waterless Shampoo Bottle

Medical Supplies
1 Bottle Alcohol
1 Bottle Peroxide
1 Bottle Iodine
1 Standard Band-Aids Box
6 2" Gauze
6 4" Gauze
4 6" Gauze
2 Pressure Bandages

2	Israeli Bandages
2	Quick Clot Gauze
2	Surgical Stapler Kit
1	Surgical Stapler Removal Kit
100	Latex Gloves
1	4.0 Silk Sutures (12 Count Box)
1	6.0 Silk Sutures (12 Count Box)
1	4.0 Nylon Sutures (12 Count Box)
1	6.0 Nylon Sutures (12 Count Box)
1	4.0 Chrome Sutures (12 Count Box)
1	6.0 Chrome Sutures (12 Count Box)
4	Saline Solution IV
2	IV Starter Kit
1	Field Surgical Kit
2	Sling
2	Tourniquet
1	Eye Patch
6	2x2 Gauze Pad
6	4x4 Gauze Pad
6	6x6 Gauze Pad
4	Syringe
1	CPR Mask
2	Emergency Blanket
1	Emergency Sleeping Bag
100	Cotton Balls
4	Surgical Tape 3/4" Roll
4	Surgical Tape 1" Roll
2	Dental Repair Kit
1	Bottle of Cloves
2	Aspirin
2	Ibuprofen
4	Halls Bag

3	Vitamin D Bottle Tablets
4	Nyquil Bottle
2	Baby Aspirin
2	4" Ace Bandage
2	6" Ace Bandage

Food

2	Black Beans 5 Gallon Bucket (36 lbs)
2	Pinto Beans 5 Gallon Bucket (36 lbs)
1	Flax seeds 2 Gallon Bucket (10 lbs)
2	Salt 2 Gallon Bucket (10lbs)
3	White Wheat Berries (ground for flour) 5 Gallon Bucket (35 lbs)
1	Vegetable Soup Mix Dehydrated (Makes 32 Gallons of Soup) 5 Gallon Bucket
2	Sugar 5 Gallon Bucket (35 lbs)
2	Long Grain Rice 5 Gallon Bucket (35 lbs)
1	Milk Replacer 5 Gallon Bucket (25 lbs)
1	Dehydrated Milk 5 Gallon Bucket (25 lbs)
1	CHICKEN Soup Base 2 Gallon Bucket (20 lbs)
1	BEEF Soup Base 2 Gallon Bucket (20 lbs)
1	HAM Soup Base 2 Gallon Bucket (20 lbs)
1	MUSHROOM Soup Base 2 Gallon Bucket (20 lbs)

1	VEGETABLE Soup Base 2 Gallon Bucket (20 lbs)
1	*CHICKEN GRAVY 2 Gallon Bucket (20 lbs)*
1	*COUNTRY BISCUIT GRAVY w / PEPPER 2 Gallon Bucket (20 lbs)*
1	Whole Egg Crystals - 7 Year Shelf # 10 Cans
3	Freeze Dried Ground Beef #10 Can
3	Freeze Dried Diced Chicken #10 Can
2	Bacon TVP #10 Can
2	Beef TVP #10 Can
2	Chicken TVP #10 Can
36	Standard Can Green Beans
36	Standard Can Peas
36	Standard Can Carrots
36	Standard Can Corn
24	Can Condensed Milk
24	Box Propel Packets (10 count)
12	Box Instant Coffee (7 count)
12	Coffee Plastic Can (2.5 Pound)
48	Canned Ham
16	Spam
36	Can Beanie Weenies
12	120 Serving Entrée Buckets from SOS Food Supply. Lowest sodium long shelf life food. Get a combination of menu A and menu B
6	120 serving Breakfast Buckets from SOS Food Supply.
60	Hydro Packs

Quantity	
60	Bottled Water (16.9 Ounce) 24 count case
12	Emergency Drinking Water (4.22 ounce pouches) 96 count case

The following is a comprehensive list of items for the second person. Obviously, if the first person has everything they need, there are some items that are not needed by the second person. Below is the list for the second person.

Quantity	Person 2
	Basic Bug In Kit
	Clothing
2	Boots
2	Coats
2	Ear Muffs
2	Full Face Mask
2	Gloves
1	Goggles
2	Hats
1	Knit Cap
2	Long Johns
4	Pants
1	Parka Pants
2	Poncho
1	Poncho Liner
1	Rain Suit
1	Rubber boots
2	Scarf
2	Shoes

12	Socks Standard
1	Tactical Vest
6	Towels
12	T-shirts
12	Underwear
6	Wool Socks

Equipment

6	Aluminum foil
2	Batteries 9 Volt 2 Pack
2	Batteries AA 6 Pack
2	Batteries AAA 8 Pack
2	Batteries C 6 Pack
2	Batteries D 6 Pack
1	Binoculars
3	Blanket Twin/Full
1	Bleach
1	Bottle Opener
2	Bowl - Plastic- Cereal
4	Bucket 5 Gallon
12	Bunge Cord
2	Camp Chairs
6	Camp Fuel
1	Can opener
24	Candles
2	Charcoal Bag Raw
1	Charcoal Lighter Fluid
1	Clothesline 100'
12	Coleman Lantern Mantles #21
	Coleman's pump repair kit
1	Lantern/Stove
1	Compass

400	Cups Plastic or Styrofoam
1	Dish Washing Brush
6	Disposable Lighter
1	Disposable Lighter - Long
3	Duct Tape - Green
3	Duct Tape - Black
1	Fishing Pole
1	Fishing Tackle Kit
1	Flashlight - Crank Up
1	Flashlight - Battery Operated
4	Gloves - All Purpose
1	Hair Scissors
1	Hand Bow Saw
4	Hand Warmer Heat Packs 10 hour
20	Hexa Pots
2	Iodine Tablets Bottle
2	Lamp Oil
24	Lamp Wicks
1	Lantern - Propane
1	Lantern Striker Lighter
24	Chem Light Sticks
1	Lighter –Butane- Refillable
2	Lighter Fluid – Butane Fuel
2	Maglite 3Watt LED 4Cell Bulb
1	Magnesium
1	Map City and County
1	Map Surrounding Cities and Counties
1	State Map
200	Waterproof Matches Package of 10
5	Standard Matches Box 200
6	Mouse Trap

1	Paper - 500 Sheet Package
400	Paper Plates
6	Paraffin Wax
12	Pen
12	Pencils
2	Pillows
	Plastic Sheeting Visqueen 3.5 MIL
2	10'x25'
	Plastic Sheeting Visqueen 4 MIL
1	3'x50'
12	Plastic Wrap
1	Playing Cards
1	Pocket Chainsaw
1	Pots & Pans Set
4	Propane – 5 gal
12	Propane Bottles– Camp Size
2	Rope 3/4" (100 feet)
1	Rubber bands (100 Count)
1	Safety Pins Box
1	Salt / Pepper Shaker
1	Scissors
2	Scotch-Brite Sponge
1	Sewing Kit
12	Sewing Needles
400	Plastic Forks
400	Plastic Knives
400	Plastic Spoons
1	Sling Shot
1	Solar Calculator
1	Spatula
1	Sta-Bil
1	Stainless Steel Bowl 3 QT

1	Stainless Steel Bowl 5 QT
1	Stainless Steel Mixing Bowl - Medium
1	Stove- Dual Fuel
12	Tarp Clip
6	Tarps (8'x10')
12	Tent Pegs
1	Tent Repair Kit
1	Thermometer 0-220 F
2	Tow Strap
4	Trash Bags – Black 2 Mil 45 Gallon
4	Trash Bags – Black 3 Mil
2	Water Bladder 5 gal E or F
1	Water Bladder Clean kit
1	Water Purification Tablets Bottle
1	Water Purifier
4	Water Purifier Ceramic Filter Element
1	WD40
12	Ziploc Bags- Gallon Box
12	Ziploc Bags- Quart Box
1	Zippo Lighter
2	Zippo Lighter Fluid - Ronsonol
2	Zippo Wick
1	Rifle
1000	Rifle Ammo
1	Shotgun
500	Shotgun Ammo
1	Pistol
1000	Pistol Ammo
1	Tactical Knife Dual Purpose
1	Rifle Spare Parts Kit

1 Shotgun Parts Kit
1 Pistol Parts Kit
2 55 Gallon Plastic Water Barrels
2 Water Tap for Plastic Barrel
  White Harvest Seed Heirloom Seed
1 Vault 30 Pouch Basic Kit

<u>Hygiene</u>
1 Chlorinating Sanitizer
1 Cocoa Butter Crème
12 Deodorant Anti-Perspirant
1 Finger Nail / Toe Nail Clippers
1 Finger Nail File
3 Floss Picks Package
1 Hair Brush
2 Hair Conditioner
9 Hair Shampoo
6 Hand Sanitizer
2 Insect Repellant 100% Deet
4 Insect Repellant Wipes
4 Lip Balm Chap Stick
12 Liquid Anti-Bacterial Soap
1 Medicated Body Powder
1 Mirror
2 Petroleum Jelly
  Prescription Medicines (30 Day
12 Supply)
2 Q-Tips 250 Count Box
24 Shaving Razors
1 Skin So Soft
24 Soap - Bars
2 Soap Dish Washing

1	Sun Block 50
96	Toilet Paper
2	Tooth Brush
1	Tooth Brush - Holder
12	Tooth Paste
12	Towelette Package Moist
12	Shower Wipes Package
4	Waterless Shampoo Bottle

Medical Supplies

1	Bottle Alcohol
1	Bottle Peroxide
1	Bottle Iodine
1	Standard Band-Aids Box
6	2" Gauze
6	4" Gauze
4	6" Gauze
2	Pressure Bandages
2	Israeli Bandages
2	Quick Clot Gauze
2	Surgical Stapler Kit
1	Surgical Stapler Removal Kit
100	Latex Gloves
1	4.0 Silk Sutures (12 Count Box)
1	6.0 Silk Sutures (12 Count Box)
1	4.0 Nylon Sutures (12 Count Box)
1	6.0 Nylon Sutures (12 Count Box)
1	4.0 Chrome Sutures (12 Count Box)
1	6.0 Chrome Sutures (12 Count Box)
4	Saline Solution IV
2	IV Starter Kit
1	Field Surgical Kit

2	Sling
2	Tourniquet
1	Eye Patch
6	2x2 Gauze Pad
6	4x4 Gauze Pad
6	6x6 Gauze Pad
4	Syringe
1	CPR Mask
2	Emergency Blanket
1	Emergency Sleeping Bag
100	Cotton Balls
4	Surgical Tape 3/4" Roll
4	Surgical Tape 1" Roll
2	Dental Repair Kit
1	Bottle of Cloves
2	Aspirin
2	Ibuprofen
4	Halls Bag
3	Vitamin D Bottle Tablets
4	Nyquil Bottle
2	Baby Aspirin
2	4" Ace Bandage
2	6" Ace Bandage

Food

2	Black Beans 5 Gallon Bucket (36 lbs)
2	Pinto Beans 5 Gallon Bucket (36 lbs)
1	Flax seeds 2 Gallon Bucket (10 lbs)
2	Salt 2 Gallon Bucket (10lbs)
3	White Wheat Berries (ground for flour) 5 Gallon Bucket (35 lbs)

	Vegetable Soup Mix Dehydrated (Makes 32 Gallons of Soup) 5
1	Gallon Bucket
2	Sugar 5 Gallon Bucket (35 lbs)
2	Long Grain Rice 5 Gallon Bucket (35 lbs)
1	Milk Replacer 5 Gallon Bucket (25 lbs)
1	Dehydrated Milk 5 Gallon Bucket (25 lbs)
1	CHICKEN Soup Base 2 Gallon Bucket (20 lbs)
1	BEEF Soup Base 2 Gallon Bucket (20 lbs)
1	HAM Soup Base 2 Gallon Bucket (20 lbs)
1	MUSHROOM Soup Base 2 Gallon Bucket (20 lbs)
1	VEGETABLE Soup Base 2 Gallon Bucket (20 lbs)
1	*CHICKEN GRAVY 2 Gallon Bucket (20 lbs)*
1	*COUNTRY BISCUIT GRAVY w / PEPPER 2 Gallon Bucket (20 lbs)*
1	Whole Egg Crystals - 7 Year Shelf # 10 Cans
3	Freeze Dried Ground Beef #10 Can
3	Freeze Dried Diced Chicken #10 Can
2	Bacon TVP #10 Can
2	Beef TVP #10 Can
2	Chicken TVP #10 Can

36 Standard Can Green Beans
36 Standard Can Peas
36 Standard Can Carrots
36 Standard Can Corn
24 Can Condensed Milk
24 Box Propel Packets (10 count)
12 Box Instant Coffee (7 count)
12 Coffee Plastic Can (2.5 Pound)
48 Canned Ham
16 Spam
36 Can Beanie Weenies
12 120 Serving Entrée Buckets from SOS Food Supply. Lowest sodium long shelf life food. Get a combination of menu A and menu B
6 120 serving Breakfast Buckets from SOS Food Supply.
60 Hydro Packs
60 Bottled Water (16.9 Ounce) 24 count case
12 Emergency Drinking Water (4.22 ounce pouches) 96 count case

About the Author

Bob Gaskin is a former Marine who has been living the Self Reliant Lifestyle for over a decade. He is 42 years old and has been married to his wife, Faith, since July of 1990. He is the owner of Black Dog Survival School.

To catch his next speaking event near you, or to email him, please visit his website at **www.blackdogsurvivalschool.com**

You can also hear him on KWTO Springfield Missouri 560 AM every Friday afternoon from 4 PM to 5 PM. If you are outside the stations area, you can listen live on KWTO's website at **www.radiospringfield.com**

Made in the USA
Lexington, KY
11 July 2015